The Russian Frontier
The Impact of Borderlands
upon the Course of
Early Russian History

The Russian Frontier

The Impact of Borderlands upon the Course of Early Russian History

Joseph L. Wieczynski

University Press of Virginia
Charlottesville

The publication of this volume is sponsored
by the VPI Educational Foundation, Inc.

THE UNIVERSITY PRESS OF VIRGINIA
Copyright © 1976 by the Rector and Visitors
of the University of Virginia

First published 1976

Library of Congress Cataloging in Publication Data

Wieczynski, Joseph L   1934–
  The Russian frontier.

  Includes index.
  1. Russia—Historical geography.   2. Frontier
thesis.   3. Frontier and pioneer life—Russia.
4. Russia—History.   I. Title.
DK18.7.W53   947   75-43753
ISBN 0-8139-0681-4

Printed in the United States of America

For
Geoffrey, Daniel, and Mary Faith
and
for Jo again

Contents

Maps

Preface

For the past several years I have explored with students and colleagues in the field of Russian studies the influence of the frontier upon the development of the early Russian state. Our speculations have ranged over a span of several centuries and have touched upon many facets of early Russian life that now are deeply obscured. As is common with such investigation, proofs for one or another of our conclusions have been difficult to devise. Quite often we have acknowledged the force of interpretations that depend upon meager source material and limited data concerning the actual conditions of the eras of history under consideration. Yet in the end we have become convinced that, despite the difficulty of substantiating particular points of our theory, the frontier played a great role in the evolution of the primitive Russian state and hitherto has been poorly appreciated as a formative influence upon the growth of the Russian nation. This work is the result of that conviction.

No part of this book is intended as a product of original research into the Russian past. My interpretation is deliberately based upon the classic accounts of Russian history elaborated by Kliuchevsky, Platonov, Presniakov, and other historians, with additional suggestions drawn from the more recent work of Philip Longworth, Paul Avrich, George Vernadsky, Robert Kerner, William McNeill, and a number of Soviet scholars. But there is so much disagreement among specialists in early Russian history that even the contentions of such eminent specialists will not be accepted by all readers. For this reason serious scholars will undoubtedly find many grounds for disagreement with particular points of this essay. But this is all to the good; for the purpose of this work is to stimulate discussion and thought on the central thesis proposed in this study. If the suggestions offered here lead scholars and students to view the early Russian past in the light in which I have cast it, then this work has served its purpose.

Many scholars have contributed in many ways to the completion of this work. I must thank particularly the three authorities on early Russia who were present at the program in Chapel Hill, North Carolina, in 1971 when I first expressed my ideas on the frontier to an audience of the Southern Conference on Slavic Studies: Professors Robert O. Crummey, Joseph T. Fuhrmann, and Walter K. Hanak. Professor

David Griffiths of the University of North Carolina not only offered valuable suggestions on that occasion but has since contributed to the development of this work. Professor Thomas Longin of Ithaca College acquainted me with some of the finer points of the frontier hypothesis elaborated by Frederick Jackson Turner. Dr. William Havard, Dean of Arts and Sciences at Virginia Polytechnic Institute and State University, has done so much to enhance my professional development that words of thanks seem paltry when measured against the debt of gratitude owed him. Professor Nicholas Riasanovsky of the University of California at Berkeley has given me encouragement by urging the completion of this work since 1971. Mr. Michael Houchens assisted me in the preparation of the manuscript and has aided my work in numerous ways. Mistakes that remain in this book should be attributed solely to the obstinacy of its author.

The method of transliteration used in this work is the modified Library of Congress system. All ligatures and diacritical marks are removed. The endings of proper names are given as "sky," not "skii" or "ski." Research for this study was supported by a grant from the Penrose Fund of the American Philosophical Society and by travel funds furnished by Virginia Polytechnic Institute and State University. I wish to thank the editors of the *Russian Review* for permission to reprint material first published in the following articles: "The Frontier in Early Russian History," *Russian Review* 31 (1972): 110–16; "Toward a Frontier Theory of Russian History," *Russian Review* 33 (1974): 284–95.

Digby Neck, Nova Scotia
August 1975

The Russian Frontier
The Impact of Borderlands
upon the Course of
Early Russian History

I.   The Frontier Hypothesis

THE TWENTIETH CENTURY seems to have bred a deep sense of humility, if not insufficiency, in scholars of all academic disciplines. The unprecedented expansion of the limits of knowledge and the tremendous accumulation of scholarly data, coupled with refinement of the critical methods of evaluating scholarly work, have led thinkers and researchers to set modest bounds for their activity and to restrict their ambitions to limits within which personal expertise can be practiced modestly but safely. Gone are the days when thinkers dared to expound complete systems of thought encompassing all being and offering keys to the understanding of all reality. Even if a new Kant or Hegel should arise, he would find his conclusions accessible only to a small circle of scholars versed in the many disciplines and vast sums of knowledge that systematic thinking now demands. Consequently, modern scholarship has prudently settled upon the monograph and the research article as chief instruments for disseminating new contributions to learning. Often these contributions are of direct benefit only to a few associates and colleagues with identical skills and specializations. Hence, the demise, at least temporarily, of the works of broad interpretation and sweeping perspective that historians of the last century often made their domain and in which they labored to create total philosophies of history.

American scholarship has produced one important exception to this reluctance to grapple with the grand designs of history. The celebrated frontier hypothesis elaborated by Frederick Jackson Turner at the turn of the century to elucidate the formative influences of American social and institutional history has a breadth of conception that allows it to be called systematic. Turner's thesis, which is probably the most renowned American contribution to the philosophy of history and certainly to American historical studies, has enlivened and molded many subsequent interpretations of the American past. Turner's theories remain vital today and, despite their many revisions and challenges, continue in use as a most original and helpful scheme for understanding the historical causes of contemporary American national life. Yet despite its heavy application by American historians, Turner's hypothesis has received scant attention by specialists in non-American history, seemingly because of their failure to discover specific instances in which Turner's views are relevant to the areas of their own professional concern.[1] Yet it would seem strange indeed if America and its institutions have developed according to a pattern of evolution that has been inoperable or inefficacious elsewhere.

The American western frontier was, according to Turner, the principal determinant of American attitudes towards the ideals of political, social, and economic life. By creating what Turner has called "the American spirit," the frontier set its stamp upon all subsequent development of the form and substance of American institutions. Turner and his successors have argued that American democracy and the American free enterprise system first arose in the American West, where the values of the intrepid frontiersman promoted a style of life and a code of personal values that emphasized personal ability and individual performance, not pedigree, inheritance, or any more aristocratic traits. In the American West life was dangerous and uncertain. The demands of everyday experience required a citizenry that could cope with instant perils, overcome a multitude of obstacles that were unknown in more settled societies, and carve a better life by mastering a vast and untamed wilderness. A man became synonymous with his abilities and skills, for upon the initiative and resourcefulness of each frontiersman depended the safety and the success of all who shared his life and work. The man who could swing an effective ax, overcome the problems of terrain and climate in his farming, organize his fellows in joint economic projects, and hold his own in a fight with enemies was the man who earned respect and following.

It was natural that as frontier societies became more settled and institutionalized, the strong and capable performer emerged as the leader of society and government. His claim to position and privilege was ability. His background, family, faith, and origins were of scant concern. In time this democratic and utilitarian approach to leadership also became institutionalized. Nothing that resembled the feudal systems of the old European world could evolve in such a milieu, for the demands of life had destroyed any predisposition toward elitism. Just as personal wealth was

[1]Several attempts have been made to apply the Turner thesis to other lands. Such efforts, however, invariably begin with an exposition of the relevance of Turner's theory to American history, then narrate the historical development of non-American societies and their borderlands with little subsequent attention to the basic principles postulated by Turner. Turner's basic notion that the frontier is a dynamic force that causes societies to evolve in one way and not in another often is ignored. We are thus left with another history of borderlands that offers no new interpretation of the national life under examination. For examples, see the various essays in *The Frontier in Perspective*, ed. Walker D. Wyman and Clifton B. Kroeber (Madison: University of Wisconsin Press, 1965). The article on Russia, "Russian Expansion in the Far East in the Light of the Turner Hypothesis," by A. Lobanov-Rostovsky, disregards any formative influence of the frontier upon Russian society and institutions.

regarded as proof of an individual's skills and virtues, prominence in politics and in the affairs of the community was the reward of ability in handling the affairs and governing the welfare of the community. Few exceptions to this general law of success were admitted on the American frontier.

While western American settlements and their inhabitants were being marked with the impress of frontier values, the vast tracts of free land available in the West provided what Turner called a "safety valve" for the more restricted populaces of the American eastern seaboard. The more resourceful and venturesome elements of the American East could trade a more serene but less rewarding way of life in their urban centers for the unlimited opportunities of the western frontier. Those who dared forsake the safety and comforts of the towns and those who elected to stake their futures upon their own resourcefulness and self-sufficiency seized the challenge of the frontier. This immense safety valve offered eastern workingmen the mobility needed to escape economic oppression and social dissatisfaction. Unlike their less fortunate counterparts in Europe, American workers could strike out toward this new land in quest of a wholly new future.

Those who exchanged their lives in the East for a new beginning on the frontier were, of course, the more volatile and restless segments of society. Their departure from the East meant the removal from American cities of social groups that were, at least in potential, a dangerous source of opposition to the values that governed the Atlantic coast of the United States. Those who remained were more pliable, more satisfied with their fates, or at least too sluggish to rebel and threaten the system that bounded their lives. They were better able to tolerate the development of aristocratic elites that transmitted their privileges almost dynastically to descendants who often lacked all quality and ability. Thus, the safety valve vented to the frontier elements of society that were so opposed to established eastern society that their continued residence in the eastern cities could only have impelled their economic and political leaders to adopt harsher and more rigid forms of control and exploitation to still their restlessness and check their manifestations of displeasure.

Once settled on the frontier, former malcontents lived a life that was incomparably freer than that known in the metropolis. The abundance of land, which could be had almost for the asking, guaranteed every man the right to work. With the cooperation of nature and the application of frugality, expertise, and hard labor, the individual homesteader could wrest from his surroundings subsistence and even abundance. The self-reliance and private enterprise of the frontiersman were enhanced by the absence of the agents of a patriarchal centralized authority. When, in time, the tax collector, the census taker, the military recruiter, and other representatives of bureaucratic control followed the settler to the frontier, the man who sought continued independence could once again draw up his roots and migrate farther westward, until the ocean finally contained his flight and closed his horizons. Indeed, some who recognized the dangers of permanent settlement traded all stability for a nomadic life among the great Rockies or the open plains of the western wilderness. Like mariners who experience true freedom only on the vast reaches of the sea, they shunned the centers of agriculture and commerce and led a solitary but unimpeded existence in regions where coercion and constraint could not reach them. Those who sacrificed their mobility and personal autonomy for the advantages of civilization they treated with contempt. For in their minds nothing could compensate a man for the loss of his right to manage his life according to his own wishes.

On the frontier local conditions nurtured a spirit of independence and individualism that precluded rigid social stratification and economic and social regimentation. But the democratic and enterprising forms of life that marked western society did not, Turner believed, remain confined to the frontier. The benefits of freer and less aristocratic forms of organization and the rewards that stemmed from an appreciation of personal accomplishment became too obvious to be ignored in any American community. The spirit of the frontier penetrated eastward and played a formative role in the evolution of national institutions. The "frontier spirit" became the "American spirit." The democracy and self-enterprise of the American West were written into the laws that guided American national growth throughout its most brilliant eras. Politics, society, and economics all felt the force of the frontier and embodied its vital features. Thus the American West became the cradle of American unicity and ensured that America did not become a carbon copy of the European lands from which the population of the United States had derived.[2]

[2]For Turner's exposition of the hypothesis see his publications: "Contributions of the West to American Democracy," *Atlantic Monthly* 89 (1903): 83–96; "Pioneer Ideals and the State University," *Indiana University Bulletin* 7 (1910): 6–29; "The Problem of the West," *Atlantic Monthly* 78 (1896): 289–97; "The Significance of the Frontier in American History," *Annual Report for the Year 1893,* American Historical Association (Washington, D.C., 1894), pp. 199–227; "The West and American Ideals," *Washington Historical Quarterly* 5 (1914): 243–57. A synopsis of the thesis and examples of its later revision can be read in *The Turner Thesis concerning the Role of the Frontier in American History,* ed. George Rogers Taylor (Boston: Heath, 1956) and *The Frontier Thesis: Valid Interpretation of American History?* ed. Ray Allen Billington (New York: Knopf, 1966). The nonspecialist seeking an introduction to Turner's work can consult these two collections with particular advantage.

The American West was so immense that its settlement and development required generations of new efforts and new migrations. Hence, the western frontier continued to function as a safety valve for decades, keeping the populace of the United States widely scattered and relieving the congestion of the cities. The natural abundance of the earth bred a contentment that offset the miscontent that often flared in the industrialized and urbanized East. Even such an inveterate enemy of democracy as Thomas Babington Macaulay was forced to admit that the American frontier played a beneficial role in the political and social development of the United States. Although he believed that democracy and free enterprise were fated someday to destroy "liberty, or civilization, or both," Macaulay conceded that America had temporarily avoided such an outcome because of its "boundless extent of fertile and unoccupied land."[3] This reprieve, he maintained, was only temporary. The exhaustion of the frontier and its dense settlement would eventually cause the dissatisfactions of the cities to spread throughout the land and give rise to new oppressive methods of halting the anarchy to which democracy must inevitably lead. Here Macaulay voiced a warning that has been expressed many times by those who link the continuation of democratic forms with the existence of a vigorous and unmastered frontier.

Turner's thesis, it is true, later attracted many critics who have questioned many of his tenets and revised his contentions in numerous new writings on the American frontier. His hypothesis has also been accused of promoting excessive American localism that ignores concomitant developments in the European world. But many of its principles have been employed with great benefit by scholars of American institutional history who also amplified some of the latent features of Turner's work by deducing additional axioms. One of the major historians who have accepted Turner's postulations and have sought further application of his suggestions was Walter Prescott Webb. Webb's treatment of the frontier thesis is important to the present study in that it effectively prepared Turner's theories for application to the history of other lands and areas of the world.

Turner had been preceded by several British and American historians who had taken cautious steps toward a frontier hypothesis. The notion of a safety valve provided by access to large tracts of free land had attracted the particular attention of some writers of the nineteenth century. A few were even prepared to admit that uninhabited or sparsely settled waste-

---

[3]William M. Tuttle, "Forerunners of Frederick Jackson Turner: Nineteenth-Century British Conservatives and the Frontier Thesis," *Agricultural History* 41 (1967): 223–24.

lands necessarily extend economic opportunity to frontiersmen and thereby prepare the soil for the emergence of the notion of political and social equality.[4] But Webb introduced something new. Concentrating less on the formative influences of the frontier than had Turner but more on the nature of frontier life and the struggle of the frontiersman with the forces that surrounded him, Webb concluded that the constant contest with nature on the frontier accounted for the dominant characteristics of the frontier mentality. Whereas struggles with one's fellowmen or with hostile political and social units demanded in society greater control, authoritarianism, and discipline, contests with nature led to increased individualism and fostered an appreciation of self-reliance that caused frontier settlements located in primitive conditions to become more democratic and self-sufficient.

In European countries that lay west and south of Poland, the term *frontier* is synonymous with the term *border,* or *boundary.* Webb noted that Europeans speak of their frontiers as dividing lines between their sovereignty and that of their neighbors, boundaries between countries having different political systems, economic orders, and ethnic origins. Americans, however, speak of their frontier as part of their national territory, "not a line to stop at, but an *area* inviting entrance."[5] American frontier movements were the entry of colonists into an area that was underpopulated but capable of tremendous exploitation. In the American West frontiersmen settled a territory that seemed limitless in its potential yet had one Indian for every six square miles of territory.[6] Although there was often hostility and conflict between the settler and the resident Indian, the primary struggle on the American frontier was not with men, but with nature. This factor Webb found crucial to the American national experience. Military confrontations with other men demand reliance upon strict regimentation, rigid organization, and unswerving obedience to the representatives of authority. The individual is subordinated to the common purpose for the sake of the preservation of the community. A social contract between the imperiled citizenry and their military authorities is necessary and usually goes unquestioned. Independent action and private initiative are viewed as dangerous to the common cause. But in the struggle with nature every man is cast upon his own resources and survives because of his skills, his fortitude, and his steadfastness in crisis. Self-reliance, not subordination, becomes the key to survival and success.

[4] Ibid., pp. 219–27.
[5] Walter Prescott Webb, *The Great Frontier* (Austin, Tex.: University of Texas Press, 1951), p. 2.
[6] Ibid., p. 3.

It was precisely this struggle with nature, Webb believed, that made the American western experience so singular that it colored all later national life and was enshrined in national laws and institutions. In the European societies from which many of the American frontiersmen had derived, life was constrained by ancient ritual, traditional laws, and established religion. Everyday existence was bounded by strict precepts that could be violated only with dire consequence. Individualism was deemed a threat to the proper functioning of the national order and was suppressed for the sake of conformity to values that were centuries old. But on the American continent settlers encountered nature. Here the fight was not against man and manmade things but against the challenges of the untamed wastelands and unfamiliar conditions:

Here were new forests, new soil, and new streams; here was new silence and immensity, too silent and extensive to be broken by a single individual or by any number then available. How small man feels in such presence. But with this consciousness of insignificance goes that of elation which comes when man feels himself blended with nature, where his vision is unobstructed and his acts unimpeded by other men. What men had done to him all his life now fell away in a single instant: nowhere was there policeman, priest or overlord to push him around. All the barricades that men had placed around him came down, and he stepped forth freer of man than he or any of his fellows had been for a very long time. Then and there he took a long step toward democracy, not political democracy but psychological, social, and economic liberty without which political democracy cannot long endure.[7]

When he conquered nature, the frontiersman felt that he could be conquered by no man. He emerged from his struggle convinced of his personal worth and determined that his society and his government should recognize and preserve that worth.

As Webb would have it, the Turner thesis thus is not applicable to all societies in the form in which Turner posed it. One may speak of new frontiers opened by overseas colonization, or by advances in technology, or by new methods of communication and transportation. But the sort of frontier that Turner studied in the American West can be found only in certain other countries, in places where expanses of wasteland, unsettled and beckoning, border on the national heartlands where settlement is denser and life is made to conform to traditions and ancient values. Although some European countries at various times in their national life had met such a condition, only one fit the Turnerian mold as well as, or

[7] Ibid., p. 31.

perhaps better than, America. That nation, which both Turner and Webb ignored in their writings, was Russia.

Before attempting to interpret early Russian history in light of the Turner and Webb theses, it will be helpful to recapitulate the basic contentions of these hypotheses. Three principles proceed from the foregoing considerations of the frontier: (1) frontier conditions encourage self-reliance, a democratic approach to political and social questions, and free enterprise; (2) free lands provide a safety valve that undercuts authoritarianism, centralization, and subordination to traditional laws and customs; (3) once frontier traits have become ingrained in the mentality of the frontiersmen, local institutions emerge that champion and protect the individual worth and freedom of activity of each citizen.

A number of corollaries can be deduced from these principles: (1) Life in the borderlands promotes greater personal initiative and self-respect, inasmuch as positive accomplishments by individuals are essential to the survival and betterment of the frontier community. (2) Struggles against the forces of nature militate against the formation of repressive social and political systems, whereas conflict with other men or alien societies leads to centralization, political and social conformity, and reliance upon military organization and the discipline it entails. (3) Agricultural work and other forms of labor that are performed within densely settled areas tend to create a system of property that demands protective institutions; other types of economic endeavor liberate men from constraints by encouraging greater mobility. (4) The existence of vast tracts of free territory along the borders of densely settled heartlands tends to attract the more adventurous and more disgruntled segments of society; these refugees organize their lives and structure their communities in ways that are usually antithetical to the settled and bureaucratic norms of life in the region from which they have fled.

One additional axiom is particularly relevant to the study of the Russian Empire during the pre-Petrine period: once frontier characteristics have determined the style of life and values of the inhabitants of borderlands, local institutions will reflect these values. The traditional center of the state will then also be influenced by these institutions (as Turner believed America to be influenced by the western frontier) and emphasize a freer, more individualistic form of life. But the state is not automatically destined to follow the example of the frontier. Strong patriarchal authorities sometimes have sufficient power and instruments of control to offset the impact of the frontier. If this course of action is adopted, then the influence of the frontier may actually promote reaction by the state and thereby become an impetus toward greater centralization, more authoritarianism, and less response to the aspirations of the citizenry. Those who are conversant with the historical growth of the Russian state will easily recognize the importance of this final consideration in the course of Russian history. Although all these principles and corollaries operated in early Russian history and some remained operative much later (and may continue even today), the triumph of the Russian state over the spirit of the Russian frontier was, as we shall see, one of the most significant victories won by the princes and Tsars of Moscow.

II. Kievan Rus: A Frontier Society

EARLY RUSSIAN HISTORY has always been a source of pride to Russian nationalists and something of a riddle to non-Russian historians. The life and institutions of the Kievan Russian state are so different from what later centuries have seen in Russian politics and society that scholars treating the earliest times of Russian development often feel that they are dealing with a totally different country. Even when compared to Western European nations of the same centuries, Kievan Rus seems unique. Free from feudal development, vigorous in international and domestic trade, dotted with urban centers that sometimes sheltered nests of learned men, Kiev seemed part of a different epoch. In trying to fathom the reasons for Kiev's unicity in the medieval world, historians have often come away from their labors with little in the way of persuasive explanations. Too often they have sought the sources of early Russian political and social forms in foreign models, usually Scandinavian, Byzantine, or German. But such comparisons generate more heat than light and fail to provide a satisfactory understanding of the earliest generations of Russian national life.

The solution to this problem becomes evident once one learns where to search for it. Early Russian chronicles and other historical writings, much like American newspapers, seldom trouble to record good news. Disasters, calamities of nature, war, riot, and rebellion are more the stuff to stimulate interest and hold an audience. Next in interest come the doings of royal persons of state and their associates, people whose loftiness and importance impart an aura of romance and excitement to even their trivial undertakings. When the land is peaceful and content, scant information on its mode of life or its successes in social and political relations are transcribed for later ages. Only when the people, either in protest of some oppression or in vengeance for some mistreatment, rise in bloody revolt and violently intrude upon the stage of history do the common folk gain admittance to historical records. At all other times they are deemed unworthy of serious attention.

So it was with early Russia. Analysis of chronicle material will never tell us whether Kievan Rus won special status in the medieval world through the efforts of its leaders or because of the work and accomplishments of its citizenry. Inasmuch as the common people were also unable to record for posterity accounts of their activity, their deeds remain unknown. And if early Russia's political and social uniqueness is to be explained by considerations of geography, all exegesis and analysis of the written word, from any source, becomes vain. Other sources and other methods of investigation must be utilized.

The most important character in Russian history has always been Russia herself. The historical development of the Russian people has been determined more by exigencies of time and space than perhaps the history of any other country. Every student of Russian history knows this as a truism. Yet historians seem reluctant to give full weight to the impact that geographical factors have had upon Russian social life. Serious works of scholarship have studied the role of rivers, the climate, and the zones of vegetation in the evolution of the Russian political and economic systems. But other peoples have been influenced by similar geopolitical considerations and have failed to manifest the peculiar characteristics that distinguish early Russian society. The contention that Kievan society was different in its institutions and in its spirit because of the interplay of unique geographical determinants is difficult to gainsay.

From the first moments of its national existence, Kievan Rus was a frontier society. Situated upon the periphery of civilization, Rus bordered upon vast lands that civilized men had always dreaded as the source of barbarism and invasion. The complex river system of what is today European Russia, dominated by the Dnieper and the Volga, attracted from all quarters freebooters and would-be conquerors who saw in these waterways a ready-made means of transportation and commerce. At the same time the natural riches and broad prospects of the southern steppe drew toward Rus nomadic barbarians whose own homelands could no longer contain their ambitions or slake their passions. On all sides the Kievan populace witnessed the surge of peoples whose primitive styles of life, work, and conquest markedly contrasted with the more settled and sedate peoples to their west. Any cohesive political unit in this area could be assured of the insecurity and tenuousness of its future. Its subjects could be certain that no ordinary manner of political and social organization could stand against the tremendous pressures from all sides. Perhaps only an amalgam of features drawn from the civilized states of the west and the nomadic neighbors of the east and south could survive and prosper in such surroundings.

Even before the rise of political and commercial centers of the Kievan state, the eastern Slavs who provided the basic ethnic stock of Rus had learned to accommodate themselves to the life and work of their neighbors. The influence of the kingdom of the Khazars was the first of several stimuli that molded eastern Slavic consciousness in its formative

FRONTIERS OF THE EARLY
RUSSIAN STATE

URAL MTS.

Pechora

N. Dvina

FINNS

Baltic Sea

ESTHS

Novgorod

Volkhov

Pskov

Lovat

Rostov Suzdal

Vladimir

oViatka

Kama

LITHUANIANS

W. Dvina

Nieman

Moscow

Riazan

BULGARS

Ural

POLES

Vistula

CARPATHIAN

MTS.

HUNGARIANS

SERBS

Deana

Chernigov

Kiev

Dnepr

Donets

Don

KHAZARS

Volga

PECHENEGS

Prut

Dniestr

Itil

Danube

BULGARIANS

Black Sea

Constantinople

Caspian Sea

CAUCASUS MTS.

BYZANTINE
EMPIRE

ARABIAN
CALIPHATE

Mediterranean Sea

0   500 Miles

stage. The Khazar capital of Itil, on the Volga, was not only a huge trading center from which commercial operations were mounted in many directions but a cosmopolitan town where people of many backgrounds mingled easily in the pursuit of their economic goals. Christians, Moslems, Jews, and pagans learned to cooperate in commercial work that benefited them all. From Itil the trade routes beckoned more intrepid enterprisers to the river systems of the Dnieper and the Volga, the Black Sea route to Constantinople, and the Caspian Way to the lands of the Arabs. During summer months those who preferred an even freer life traded the security of the capital for a nomadic and highly individualistic life along the steppe, where all authority, even that of Itil, was weak.[1] Slavs who were subjected to the military control of the Khazars found themselves exposed thereby to the advantages of the Khazar occupations and eventually were drawn into the economic activity upon which the strength of the Khazars depended. In this process, the eastern Slavs were introduced to a form of national organization that was distinct on all counts from the feudal and manorial systems that would continue to suppress private initiative and personal mobility in Europe for centuries.

With the formation of the Kievan state and the decline of the Khazar kingdom, the eastern Slavs found themselves cast into the role of successor to their former mentors. The fragile political order of Rus was forced to combat the nomadic forces that had beset the Khazar kingdom until its final collapse. But appreciation of the commercial successes of the Khazars determined the economic activity of the people of Rus for centuries. Learning from their former masters and teachers, the early Russians constructed a system of trade even more ambitious and more rewarding than what had flowed through Itil. The personal enterprise and self-sufficiency that such trade demanded, coupled with the individual bravery and self-reliance that the constant struggle with raiders of the steppe bred into the citizenry of Kievan Rus, produced a subject who was little inclined to acknowledge limitations of his personal mobility or restriction of his private life. As early Russian institutions arose, it was natural that they should reflect the psychology of those whom they were designed to serve. These institutions, as we shall see, were as colored by the circumstances of frontier life as were the people of Rus.

It is not difficult to discover the impact of the frontier upon the early Kievan state. Seemingly all aspects of economic life were fraught with peril during the Kievan period. Those who conducted trading operations along the river system that emptied into the Black Sea faced the constant

[1]James Mavor, *An Economic History of Russia,* 2d ed. (New York: Russell and Russell, 1965), 1: 12.

danger of attack from nomadic rivals, first the Pechenegs, later the Polovtsy, as well as dangers mounted by the rivers themselves. The famous account from the mid-tenth century by the Byzantine emperor Constantine Porphyrogenitus illustrates some of the perils faced by Kievan commercialists who sailed the Dnieper River. The hardships encountered while passing the various "barrages," or cataracts, of the Dnieper drained the energy of the Russian traders and their attendants, leaving them weakened for their contests with mortal opponents. Pecheneg tribesmen followed the passage of the Russian convoys and bided their time, awaiting opportunities for attacks that would bring them the booty stored in the Russian ships. The merchants were well aware of the points at which they could expect ambushes from the Pechenegs and were ever conscious of the unseen eyes that followed their progress.[2] To protect their valuable trade with the Byzantines, Kievan princes positioned large armies along the vulnerable points of the river route and maintained them in place until the safety of the merchants and their wares was assured.[3] But such precautions were effective only for part of the journey. The Pechenegs (and their later successors on the steppe, the Polovtsy) continued to follow their quarry from cover, seeking a suitable moment to attack or hoping for a disaster that would place the Russian traders, their slaves, and their goods at their mercy. Independent bands of pirates also harassed the Russian travelers, competing with the more organized Pechenegs and Polovtsy for Russian riches.[4] Even after these convoys had reached the open waters of the Black Sea, their perils were not at an end. Forced to hug the northern coasts because of fierce storms that were likely to arise without warning, the Russian ships were accompanied along their route by nomadic warriors who rode along the shore and carefully followed the passage of the Russians, hoping for a storm or a wreck that would drive their ships to shore, where they could be plundered.[5]

But these southern raiders made their mark upon many other facets of Kievan national life. The history of Rus is a single, almost unbroken record of conflict with these tribes, a protracted engagement that fell most heavily upon the agricultural communities of the southern Kievan borderlands and the hunters and other enterprisers who plied their

[2]Constantine Porphyrogenitus, *De administrando imperio*, ed. Gy. Moravcsik, trans. R. J. H. Jenkins (Budapest, 1949), pp. 57–63.

[3]S. M. Soloviev, *Istoriia Rossii s drevneishikh vremen* (Moscow, 1960–62), 1: 524.

[4]Ibid., p. 525.

[5]V. O. Kliuchevsky, *History of Russia*, trans. C. J. Hogarth (New York: Russell and Russell 1960), 1: 85.

various trades along the steppe. One Soviet scholar has calculated that between 915 and 1036 the princes of Kiev waged sixteen major wars against the Pechenegs, irrespective of minor military clashes that were too commonplace to mention.[6] Early in the tenth century the Kievan princes erected systematic emplacements of entrenchments and stockades on the southern and southwestern approaches to the Kievan state in order to deter the incursions of these enemies.[7] These wars were waged in areas that were especially attractive to Russian farmers, part of the region that later became known as the black earth belt of the Ukraine. Abundant crops and a climate that was usually more beneficent than that known farther north had lured many individuals who depended for their subsistence upon their annual harvests. As steppe warfare increased in intensity, many of these frontiersmen were killed, robbed, or carried into slavery by marauding raiders. Those who survived ran similar risks that increased as Russian defenses in the south proved inadequate to restrain these depredations.

Russian chronicles vividly depict the devastations and hardships visited upon these southern frontiersmen at the end of the eleventh and beginning of the twelfth centuries. Towns and villages lay in waste. Meadows where cattle and horses had grazed in herds along the steppe lay desolate. Exhausted by hunger and the relentless struggle for survival, Russian farmers began to surrender to the enemy out of desperation. "A multitude of Christian people were thus led away to an unknown land, sorrowing, tormented, stiff with cold, hungry and thirsty and miserable, their faces pinched and their bodies black, their tongues inflamed, naked and barefoot, their feet pierced with thorns."[8] The Polovtsy, like the Mongols who were to follow them later, made constant incursions into Rus to obtain booty and slaves, without any real desire to destroy the state or bend it to their will. They primarily sought "live goods," captives who could be enslaved and sold to merchants from Venice and the East, who were ready to deal with anyone for this valuable human treasure.[9] Those who lived within the range of the onslaughts of the Polovtsy learned to cope with dread and the realization that their own resourcefulness and abilities were the best guarantee of their continued survival.

Although the most spectacular and most costly wars of Kievan Rus were conducted along the southern borderlands, the entire state was not

[6] Boris Grekov, *Kiev Rus* (Moscow, 1959), p. 626.
[7] Kliuchevsky, *History,* 1: 86.
[8] George Vernadsky et al., *A Source Book for Russian History from Early Times to 1917* (New Haven: Yale University Press, 1972), 1: 30–31.
[9] George Vernadsky, *Kievan Russia* (New Haven: Yale University Press, 1948), p. 224.

far removed from theaters of warfare. In the north, Russian princes campaigned against Finnish and Lithuanian tribesmen. In the northeast the Volga Bulgars often attacked Russian holdings and in 1088 were so successful in their endeavors that they wrested from the control of Rurikid princes the town of Murom. In the west the Poles proved a formidable and constant foe, as they would remain for centuries thereafter. Restless and independent Slavic tribes who had not yet submitted to Russian power, such as those who had settled in the Pomorie, resisted Rurikid rule and violently fought to preserve their native customs and way of life. Even when neighboring tribes were defeated and settled as tributaries within the boundaries of the Kievan state, their wild and unconquerable spirit was likely to provoke domestic disorder through bloody rebellions against their overlords and reprisals against the populace that attempted to assimilate them.[10]

Yet a curious fact emerged from all this turmoil, a fact that was to be repeated time and again in subsequent Russian history. It quickly became obvious that whenever a modicum of assurance could be had that certain borderlands were not totally inhospitable to life and work, sizeable numbers of Russian settlers preferred such frontier conditions to continued residence in areas closer to the seats of central power and more limiting to personal liberty. During the reign of Yaroslav the Wise, one of the main points of defense against the Polovtsy was the region of the river Rhos, south of the town of Kiev. Here Yaroslav commanded that captured Lech tribesmen be pressed into service as mercenaries, comprising a military border guard. As soon as the Lech had ensured that the Polovtsy could no longer raid at their pleasure, they were joined by emigrants from the interior sectors of Rus who seemed to prefer the rigors and uncertainty of frontier life to their more settled but apparently less rewarding existence elsewhere. These in turn were joined by Pecheneg warriors who had transferred their allegiance to Kiev after their defeat by Sviatoslav. Turks and other non-Russian peoples now in the Kievan service also appeared in their community. These dissimilar groups formed a nomadic military garrison that grazed herds on the steppe during the summer and secured themselves in fortified outposts during the winter. Because their style of life and values seemed to approximate the barbarous Polovtsy, whom they opposed, Russians referred to the members of this community as *svoi pagani,* "our own pagans," even though they remained predominantly Christian and had their own cathedral in the town of Yuriev. These frontiersmen continued their incessant struggle against the Polovtsy until the crumbling of southern defenses brought

[10]Soloviev, 1: 368.

about their destruction. By the twelfth century the area in which they had settled had been reduced to a wasteland.[11]

Other inhabitants of Kievan Rus faced dangers, sometimes on a daily basis, that often were as terrible as those that threatened inhabitants of war zones and those engaged in the arduous commercial operations. From north to south the Russian peasant contended with an unbenevolent nature to wrest his crops from the earth, braving great extremes of temperature, uncertain harvests, the raids of enemies, and the knowledge that a poor yield could mean death by starvation. Those whose affairs kept them behind the relative safety of town walls found themselves dependent for their food, defense, and livelihood upon those who lived in remote regions and were affected by a multitude of uncertainties. Monks and other ecclesiastics wrestled with the inbred paganism and stubborn barbarism of their primitive flocks, all the while carving from the wilderness their monasteries and other enclaves of civilization and Christian morality. Throughout the Russian north traders from their center at Novgorod competed with uncivilized or semicivilized natives for valuable furs, suffering extreme cold and deprivation in a land that provided little subsistence.

Even in such a cosmopolitan and commercialized municipality as Novgorod the Great, citizens experienced on a first-hand basis the struggle for survival. The chronicle of Novgorod recounts a number of dire years in which terrible disasters followed one another as though determined to break the spirit of the townspeople. In 1128, for example, a great famine so reduced the townsfolk to desperation that they were driven to eat leaves, moss, pulp, straw, and whatever else came to hand, while death from starvation and disease was rampant throughout the principality. A great flood that accompanied the famine carried off many more victims.[12] It is hardly surprising that the people of Novgorod sought the reason for their tribulations in the appearance of comets and other physical phenomena that might explain the physical and mental travail through which they passed with such regularity.

In the presence of such suffering, danger, and precariousness, every man was put upon his mettle. Those who could not react positively to any test with celerity and acumen could not long survive the trying ordeals that were endemic to this frontier society. Those who relied upon patriarchal authorities for their preservation often found them unable to save their subjects. But those who accepted the challenge of their environment

[11] Kliuchevsky, *History*, 1: 190.
[12] *The Chronicle of Novgorod*, trans. Robert Michell and Nevill Forbes (Hattiesburg, Miss.: Academic International Press, 1970), p. 11.

and strove to meet it headlong not only won for themselves personal gain and individual satisfaction but often the recognition and respect of their fellows. In troubled times no one is more important than the man who can withstand adversity and devise strategies for mastering it. It was natural that such strong individuals should acquire economic power, social recognition, and often political power. Analysis of the social and political structure of Kievan Rus reveals most clearly that strong performers comprised the privileged elite of the state, an aristocracy of ability that garnered and retained its status through demonstrated ability and records of accomplishment. At the same time, strong princely power was all but unknown while Kievan Rus was at the height of its power, before the disastrous internecine strife of the later eleventh and twelfth centuries.

In an age when the idea of strong kingly power was first beginning to arise in Europe, the authority of Russian princes, including that of the grand prince, was slight. Few Russian princes of the tenth and eleventh centuries dared suggest that their power rested upon anything more than the skill with which they acquitted themselves in the interests of their subjects. A prince who ignored this principle of accountability or who simply proved unsatisfactory in the discharge of his duties often found himself driven from office by the people of his principality. Novgorod the Great, where the power of the prince was particularly weak, led the way in restricting the purview of supreme authorities. The notion that the prince served for definite purposes and was to be retained for his personal achievements toward the benefit of the principality was axiomatic in Novgorod. The chronicle reports that in 1136 the men of Novgorod filed formal charges against their prince, Vsevolod, for his failure to care properly for the lower social elements of the town and for his vacillation in battle. Obviously the prince was expected to show social concern and excel in economic management and military prowess. Because he had lacked distinction in these areas, the people of the town "showed him the road," as chroniclers of Novgorod liked to term the dismissal of their princes.[13]

Insurrection against ineffective princes was also exercised at the center of the state, in Kiev itself. In 1068, when the Polovtsy first attacked Rus, the prince of Kiev, Iziaslav I, poorly organized the defenses of the town against this new menace. For this reason the men of Kiev "held an assembly on the marketplace" and urged the prince to undertake a vigorous policy against the invaders. When Iziaslav either failed to follow their instructions or again disappointed the townspeople in battle with the

[13]Ibid., p. 14.

Polovtsy, the town of Kiev rebelled against him, drove him off to other lands (he later sought refuge in Poland), and proclaimed as his successor Prince Vseslav of Polotsk. But Vseslav proved cowardly in later clashes with the barbarians, whereupon the men of Kiev had no qualms in admitting that even Iziaslav had been a better commander. Prince Iziaslav was invited to return to his position as grand prince and agreed to do so.[14]

A half-century later the men of Kiev had acquired no greater tolerance for a disappointing prince. In 1113 the townspeople of Kiev sought a strong leader who could contain and chastise quarreling local princes, whose debilitating civil wars were ruining the Kievan economy and causing adverse changes in its social structure. They therefore invited Prince Vladimir Monomakh to assume the position of grand prince, following the death of its incumbent. As is well known, Prince Vladimir declined the offer out of fear that his acceptance would violate the normal order of succession and occasion new domestic violence. The men of Kiev did not respond kindly to any prince who thought his own judgment superior to theirs. They manifested their displeasure by rising in rebellion, plundering the palace of a local official, and attacking and robbing Jews. The town then informed Vladimir that, should he continue to ignore their summons, they would attack other officials, beat Vladimir's sister-in-law, and commit other outrages against local monasteries. The prince was told that these deeds of violence would be his responsibility, inasmuch as they were caused by his refusal to honor the desires of the people.[15] Violence has always been the traditional method by which frontiersmen have expressed their wishes to their authorities. Here we encounter an example of how the common folk of any society gain the attention of chroniclers when they temporarily put aside their usual occupations for more violent activities.

The princes of Rus were also restricted in their power by their boyars and other high-ranking advisers and assistants. From the very earliest Kievan times the principle was established that the boyars shared with the prince responsibility for government and the defense of the state. In the year 945 the boyars, as well as "the whole people of Rus," are mentioned in the treaty between Prince Igor and the Byzantine emperor, Ro-

[14] *The Russian Primary Chronicle: Laurentian Text,* trans. and ed. Samuel Hazard Cross and Olgerd P. Sherbowitz-Wetzor (Cambridge, Mass.: Mediaeval Academy of America, 1953), pp. 148–50.
[15] Vernadsky et al., 1: 32. The urban citizens of Kievan Rus also were predisposed to set aside the claims of senior princes in favor of junior members of the princely line. In this manner they hoped to weaken princely power still further and extract for themselves additional privileges and independence. See M. N. Tikhomirov, *The Towns of Ancient Rus* (Moscow: Foreign Languages Publishing House, 1959), pp. 230–32.

manus, apparently to demonstrate both to the Byzantines and to the Russian people that Igor was acting in accordance with the wishes of his subjects and not on his own authority.[16] Boyars were consulted at least concerning the most important issues of foreign policy thereafter, nor was their say in this important area merely honorary. The boyars were also allowed to express their opinion on what proved to be the single most important decision made by the prince in Kievan times. When Prince Sviatoslav considered the possibility of converting the land to Christianity, the boyars were asked to debate the matter. Their refusal to approve conversion caused Rus to remain pagan for another generation. Grand Prince Vladimir later secured the agreement of his boyars before ordering the conversion of Rus to the Christian faith in or about 988.[17] The princes of Rus acknowledged that their power rested upon a popular mandate until the influence of the boyars was undermined by the autocratic policies of Prince Andrew Bogoliubsky and his successors in the lands of the Russian northeast.

The notion that the prince was expected to consult his boyars on crucial matters became institutionalized in Rus. While the prince of Kiev resided in his capital, he customarily received the advice of his boyars on a daily basis, early each morning. Chronicles detail some of the issues on which the opinion of the boyars was sought. Military affairs and the relations between the grand prince and his brother princes were most often discussed and debated. The defense of the land "against pagans," the feasibility of launching military operations against the steppe and against other principalities was studied and resolved. The routes to be followed on such campaigns, the timing and content of peace treaties and similar matters also received boyar comment. Boyars also participated with the prince in the administration of justice, negotiations with foreigners, enactment of new legislation, the disposition of the principality following the prince's death, and regulation of the laws of succession to office.[18] When convocations of Russian princes were held, no prince felt free to resolve any vital matter without first seeking the consent of his boyars. The grand prince himself could not order a subordinate prince to undertake a military campaign, even for the good of the entire state, if the boyars of the prince in question opposed that action. By the same token, princes were constrained to pursue courses of action they personally deemed infeasible or unrewarding whenever the boyars judged such actions differently.[19]

[16]*Russian Primary Chronicle,* p. 74.
[17]Vernadsky, *Kievan Russia,* p. 182.
[18]V. O. Kliuchevsky, *Boiarskaia duma drevnei Rusi,* 3d ed. (Moscow, 1902), pp. 43–44.
[19]Ibid., pp. 51–52.

Yet these impressive prerogatives and privileges did not bestow upon the boyars anything resembling permanent social supremacy. In Kievan times the boyars enjoyed no more political or legal rights than did other classes. Class privileges and legal sanctions were not allurements the princes extended to secure the cooperation of the boyars, for such a notion was repugnant to the very spirit of Kievan society. Individuals could join the ranks of the boyars by rendering effective service to a prince, by acquiring great wealth, by obtaining extensive holdings of land, or by otherwise demonstrating their personal worth and ability. Social antecedents seemingly played little role in the process of winning boyar status.[20]

Conversely, individuals could be stripped of boyar rank at the will of the prince, most often for dereliction of duty or for inability to render satisfactory service. Boyar status could not be transmitted hereditarily to one's children. Each individual had to prove himself to win that title, which was personally bestowed by the prince. During the tenth and eleventh centuries most boyars seem to have held their high positions only for a few years. Privileged, aristocratic clans were unknown in Kievan Rus, and Rus had no knowledge of, or practical use for, the coats of family arms that could frequently be seen among the Polish aristocracy from early times.[21] The idea that boyar standing was conditional upon personal ability and continued performance remained strong late into Kievan history. By the end of the twelfth century a number of serving families had secured such high position and privilege that their members automatically were granted boyar rank in various princely courts when they had attained a required age. But even then, when Kiev was in full decline and Kievan society was in disarray, chronicles report that among these aristocratic servitors could be found some boyars who had originated from the lowest social strata. Some were children of the common clergy, while others were of peasant birth.[22] The highest positions in society remained open to enterprising men of intelligence and skill until the Mongol invasion.

The power of the princes and the boyars was further checked by the popular town assembly of Kievan Rus, the *veche*. Every student of the Russian past knows the prominent role played by the veche in local and national politics, particularly in the principality of Novgorod. At one time or another, however, strong veches emerged in many other Russian towns. The veche of Smolensk was so powerful that it approved treaties during wartime, set the amount of tribute paid the prince, and ratified

[20]Vernadsky, *Kievan Russia*, p. 140.

[21]See the remarks of Werner Philipp, *Russia's Position in Medieval Europe: Essays in History and Literature* (Leiden: Brill, 1972), pp. 28–29.

[22]Kliuchevsky, *Boiarskaia duma*, p. 56.

grants of land and privileges to notables.[23] By the mid-twelfth century the veche of Polotsk had clearly limited the authority of its prince and made his tenure dependent upon the approval of the veche. In 1138 the veche of Chernigov determined a vital issue of foreign policy by forcing its prince to conclude peace with Prince Yaropolk, thereby ending an unpopular war.[24] High officials of the church were also subject to control by the veche, not only in Novgorod, where such circumstances were usual and well recorded, but elsewhere throughout the Kievan realm. Saint Cyril of Turov obtained his appointment as bishop of that town only after petitioning the office from the prince and the veche.[25] Where the veche was powerful, it wielded its authority indiscriminately over the dignitaries of church and state.

In speaking of the veche, however, one ought not to suppose that the assembly of townspeople was a highly formal institution with set hours of meeting and a designated place for convention. Although the veche of some towns did meet in a set location, in other places the veche often assembled when and where it was needed or whenever it wished to express an opinion on important happenings. Princes whose power was especially dependent upon the continued support and approval of the townsmen frequently convoked the veche on the spur of the moment, to avoid making decisions that later might prove unpopular. On some occasions veche meetings between the prince and the townsfolk took place with all mounted and prepared for military action.[26] In such instances the veche resembled meetings of an armed populace with its military commanders, similar to the popular militias that worked the salvation of the Russian state during the final stages of the Time of Troubles. Far from being a dry and bureaucratic instrument of popular participation in government, the veche was a dynamic and fluid means of fathoming the will of the people on questions vital to the welfare of the entire principality. The veche existed because to ignore the popular will was a clear violation of the principle of accountability in government. Violation of this canon was a step that few princes and their boyars dared take before the end of the eleventh century, and only rarely and carefully in the next century.

Like its political structure, the social structure of Kievan Rus was variegated to a degree unknown elsewhere in Western societies of the

[23]P. V. Golubovsky, *Istoriia Smolenskoi zemli do nachala XV st.* (Kiev, 1895), pp. 214–15; Tikhomirov, p. 217.

[24]Tikhomirov, pp. 214–16, 227.

[25]N. K. Nikol'sky, *Materialy dlia istorii drevnerusskoi dukhovnoi pis'mennosti* (Saint Petersburg, 1907), p. 63.

[26]Kliuchevsky, *Boiarskaia duma,* pp. 43–44.

time. Until at least the early twelfth century, Rus was an extremely healthy social organism marked by considerable social mobility. It has been estimated that not less than 13 percent of the populace of Rus resided in the towns.[27] If this is so, the Russian middle class (the so-called *liudi*) comprised a proportionately large segment of early Russian society. Although these individuals were obliged to discharge obligations and fulfill duties for their princes, the towns, and the nobility, they were not constrained by personal bondage of any type. Below this middle class in the social hierarchy lay the quite large class of free farmers. Members of this stratum were arranged according to levels determined by fiscal and other obligations to towns and lords, but their personal freedom was unquestioned. Only at the base of the Russian social pyramid could the indentured and the slaves be found; and even these had not completely lost the hope of recovering their personal emancipation and the dream of undertaking a new life.

Most of the slaves of Kievan society were prisoners of war for whom ransom could not be collected from their people. As Kiev began to decline, however, more and more native Russians appeared among them, usually peasants who were forced to sell themselves into indenture or permanent bondage out of economic necessity or to secure the protection of local strongmen (who almost invariably were large landowners) against the marauding Polovtsy or other raiders. Until the time of Yaroslav the Wise (1019–1054), full slavery could be imposed upon a man only in three circumstances. A person could voluntarily sell himself into perpetual bondage to repay a debt or obtain the means of his subsistence. A man who married a female slave without first securing from her master a guarantee of his own continued freedom would become the property of the woman's owner. Anyone who agreed to serve another as steward or housekeeper would also become the chattel of that person.[28] In no other way could a man be deprived of his personal liberty.

Early Russian law was careful to allow slaves the opportunity to repay the debt that determined their bondage and thereby regain free status. Even prisoners of war did not usually remain permanent slaves. Ransom always ensured the immediate release of foreign prisoners. But even those unable to secure such ransom did not remain in eternal servitude. Rather, such captives were forced to labor for their masters until their work yielded value equal to the amount that their ransom would have provided. Although this provision may have been violated at various times and in

---

[27] Vernadsky, *Kievan Russia*, p. 140.
[28] George Vernadsky, *Medieval Russian Laws* (New York: Octagon Books, 1947), p. 52.

various parts of Rus, Yaroslav's code of law, the *Russkaia Pravda,* does not mention military captivity as a condition for full slavery.[29] Here the idea of the personal worth of individuals extended even to the benefit of the most unfortunate members of early Russian society and embraced even those who recently were part of the nomadic hordes that so devastated and terrorized the borderlands of Rus. It is also significant that, although slaves were numerous in Kievan Rus and were important to the economy both as a labor force and as an article of commerce, there is no record of a single slave uprising during Kievan times. In other societies, where the condition of slaves was worse, such uprisings were commonplace and often terrible in their consequences.[30]

Because of these considerations, extensive social mobility must have been a prevalent and accepted fact in Kievan Rus, particularly before the eruption of the disastrous civil wars of the late eleventh and twelfth centuries. It was undoubtedly possible, at least in isolated instances, for a man to rise from the ranks of the indentured bondmen through the class of free farmers to the middle class, acquiring increased status, wealth, and influence as he progressed. Once having become members of the middle class, individuals who were unusually gifted and enterprising gained the opportunity to secure wealth, particularly if they associated themselves with those who directed the lucrative trading operations. Inasmuch as Russian princes were accustomed to conferring boyar rank upon those whose personal successes demonstrated their adroitness in managing their affairs, the former bondman could even contemplate an invitation to boyar status, which would bring him to the pinnacle of the Kievan social and political system and accord him power and privileges. Throughout Kievan times the Russian church often enjoined masters to free their slaves and bondmen. We cannot believe that this call went completely unheeded and can assume that individuals (or perhaps families over the span of several generations) were able to rise from the unfree depths of Kievan society to the very ranks of the boyars. It is also reasonable to suppose that the exchange of individuals between the class of free farmers and the middle class was frequent. Those who wished to leave the land for other occupations could do so readily. Those who found that their affairs in the towns did not prosper could retreat to the countryside, where the availability of free land, especially in outlying areas, provided a form of social security that guaranteed a man his subsistence. No other medieval society approached Kiev in the mobility and opportunity afforded its citizens.

[29] Vernadsky, *Kievan Russia,* pp. 149–50.
[30] Grekov, *Kiev Rus,* p. 346.

The interaction of the frontier best explains the great social mobility that characterized Kievan Rus, the freedom and autonomy enjoyed by many of its farmers, the large and dynamic middle class, and the appreciation of personal ability that allowed a man to attain even the most exalted positions in society and politics. The social conditions created by the frontier in turn fostered in the citizens of the Kievan state a spirit of self-reliance that enhanced their own appreciation of their worth and bred in them scant appreciation of more rigid and doctrinaire forms of organization. Because the early Russian state was exposed to the frontier in many directions along borders that melted into broad expanses of wilderness, many of its inhabitants were thoroughly familiar with the demands and the joys of frontier life. Self-reliance, individualism, and a predisposition to democratic methods developed across the entire state and were not limited to those who dealt in outlying sectors.

The frontier made its presence felt at the very center of the nation, where its formative influence can be seen in early Russian political and social forms. Was it not the frontier that gave rise to the veche, particularly in the lands of the Russian northwest, where the great tracts of land controlled by Novgorod provided a safety valve that stimulated free enterprise and fostered a democratic approach to political life? Even in aristocratic circles the frontier spirit prevailed. There is no need to search Byzantine or Scandinavian models for explanations of the power won by the boyar duma in early Kiev at the expense of the prince. The concept of shared responsibility and joint venture so prevalent in all frontier societies here made its incursion into the highest reaches of political life. The inclination of frontiersmen to select the best man for any given job and to reward him accordingly was probably responsible also for the Russian practice of alloting service-tenure estates to those best able to render service to the state. At the same time, the relatively slight incidence of indenture and bondage throughout the Kievan realm can probably best be explained by the still unconquered and unsettled frontier lands that stretched away to the east, the north, and the south of the Kievan state. For although commerce brought Rus its quickest and most substantial profits, agricultural work remained the occupation of the bulk of the populace. The unsettled frontier lands provided a safety valve that averted dense settlement in the Russian countryside. The free farmer could escape incipient bondage by fleeing to uninhabited wastelands, where the struggle with nature would replace conflict with one's fellowmen. In a land where vicissitudes of climate and frequent acts of violence threatened the mode of production upon which all life depended, it was more rational to allow malcontents to carry on productive work in virgin lands than to reduce them to chattel.

Had Frederick Jackson Turner applied his frontier hypothesis to Rus, he surely would have concluded that the frontier also brought the Kievan state its great interest in commerce. The frontier quickly creates a need for merchants and encourages the success of commercial agents who can supply border areas with their basic needs rapidly and without reliance upon foreign economies that are far removed.[31] Once the intricacies of commercial operations have been mastered at home, it is far easier to apply their principles abroad, where Kievan merchants were able to win the great profits that gave Rus its sound economic foundation. In short, Rus became a unique medieval state because of the uniqueness of its surroundings.

[31]See Turner's comments on this point in Billington, ed., *The Frontier Thesis*, p. 13.

III.   The Decline of Kiev and the Survival of the Frontier Lands of Novgorod

THE GEOGRAPHY OF the Kievan Russian state was such that mobility, free enterprise, and private economic activity not only were facilitated but, in many instances, became prerequisites for anyone seeking more of life than the barest essentials of food, lodging, and property. The principality of Novgorod, the northernmost of the many principalities of Rus, was perhaps more determined by its environment and climate than any other Russian princedom. The town of Novgorod and its immediate hinterland lay far beyond the most densely settled regions of the Kievan heartland. Hindered by a climate that was all but totally inhospitable to dependable agricultural pursuits, Novgorod was fortunate in the many natural riches that abounded in the forests and bodies of water that profusely covered its territory.[1] Wild animals, many bearing valuable furs, fish, and forest products of every sort were copious in the environs of the towns and, as the men of Novgorod soon discovered, were even more plentiful eastward and northward of the main center of settlement. Because agriculture was risky during most years and impossible during the long winters, Novgorod quickly turned to the exploitation of the natural riches of its forests and waters. But the original territory of Novgorod was soon exhausted of its treasures. Trappers and fishermen were forced to enter new and virgin wastelands, colonizing the lands about the Northern Dvina River and the White Sea and sending exploratory expeditions to the Pechora River and the foothills of the northern ranges of the Ural Mountains.

The uncharted lands and waters of the arctic region were discovered to be rich in birds, fish and fur-bearing animals. By the twelfth century the exploration, colonization, and exploitation of these regions secured for the town of Novgorod an immense northern empire that rolled away to the Urals in the east and the shores of the arctic seas in the north.[2] Far removed from any reminder of civilization, the hunters, trappers, and fishermen of Novgorod found it impossible to establish permanent settlements in these new territories, largely because of the absence of arable land. Instead, they lived a completely nomadic existence, using their comparatively sophisticated military skills and their relatively advanced

---

[1]A. I. Nikitsky, *Istoriia ekonomicheskaia byta velikago Novgoroda* (Moscow, 1893), p. 5.
[2]S. F. Platonov, *Proshloe russkogo severa* (Berlin, 1924), pp. 16–18.

weaponry to subdue the primitive tribesmen who inhabited these parts. Conquered tribesmen were forced to acknowledge the authority of Novgorod, a condition that allowed the colonists to impose upon them tribute, which usually was paid in the form of expensive furs. Occasionally Novgorod assisted its departed brethren with full military expeditions that broke the feeble resistance of local tribal leaders. But the work of maintaining the subdued tributaries and collecting the animal tribute remained the occupation of the private enterprisers and commissioned agents who had first explored these regions.[3] Those who thirsted for personal freedom and complete independence from the regulations of central authorities found here unlimited opportunities to elaborate a democratic way of life founded upon the principle of free enterprise.

But the lust for adventure and the desire for even greater profit drove settlers from Novgorod far beyond the boundary of lands known in the town of Novgorod. Once explored areas that lay nearer the town of Novgorod had been subdued and exploited with regularity, the men of Novgorod dispatched armed bands to broaden the scope of their operations. Even before the Mongol invasion of Kievan Rus, expeditions from Novgorod crossed the northern Ural Mountains and attempted to appropriate the lands that stretched eastward, lands that were rich not only in animal life and furs but in valuable sources of raw materials. Thus occurred the first Russian exploration of northern Siberia. But here the vigor of Novgorod finally met its match. Local natives were better organized and more hostile than their counterparts on the western side of the Urals. Many bands of Novgorodians who undertook these expeditions failed to return to their homeland. Larger military detachments sent from Novgorod suffered a similar fate.[4] Reluctantly, further operations beyond the Urals were terminated.

The vast empire that Novgorod created along these northern frontiers brought the principality raw wealth that ensured her future as a great trading center, a role that culminated in Novgorod's entry into the Hanseatic League. These commercial operations in turn led to the emergence in Novgorod of a sizeable middle class, in which success was always the result of personal accomplishment and where appreciation of the values of private enterprise became deeply rooted. The notion that the principality should be administered by those whose ability and energy were responsible for its economic success was widely accepted. Of all the Russian towns, Novgorod most restricted the power of the prince and strictly delimited the areas of his authority. The town preferred to main-

[3] Ibid., pp. 25–26.
[4] For an example, see *Chronicle of Novgorod*, pp. 36–37.

tain a prince only in the capacity of commander of the armed forces. Indeed, the prince of Novgorod was not allowed to keep his residence within the walls of the town, lest he develop a proprietary sense of his role in Novgorod's affairs. Even such a renowned champion of Novgorod's independence as Prince Alexander Nevsky was "shown the road" by his subjects, once his military victory over the Swedes was secure. The normal activities of the political and economic life of the principality were directed by the veche, in which the leading merchant families and other notables comprised an influential group that could use its money and persuasion to guarantee legislation favorable to its interests.

The empire of Novgorod was a classic frontier society. Extending vast distances into regions that were largely uninhabited, it hardly resembled a political unit in any known sense. Long after its colonization was complete, the population remained sparse, with the only sites of community life limited to scattered defensive garrisons and far-flung trading posts. Its citizens were, as one scholar has remarked, "a population in motion most of the time."[5] Although the first explorers of the regions of the White Sea and the Arctic Ocean were boyars and prosperous merchants from the town of Novgorod, these were soon followed by peasants and other simple folk who settled among the native Karelians and other natives on land that was so abundant that there is no mention in history of conflict over its possession.[6] Here was a safety valve of such immensity that any man wishing to chance the rigors of farming in the north could become a homesteader with no difficulty whatsoever.

From their earliest appearance in the north the peasants of Novgorod organized their activities in democratic manner and founded their communities upon the principles of the egalitarian *mir* and *volost*. These institutions, which were directed by officials and elders elected by the peasantry, oversaw the free use of pastures, waters, and woodland and ensured that each peasant family paid its share of taxation to the principality. Equal opportunity and fair access to local lands and wildlife were also supervised. In short, these bodies were instruments of self-government designed to preserve the interests and opportunities of each farmer.[7] The higher officials of Novgorod were content to allow these peasants such independence, knowing well that their productivity would

[5] Robert J. Kerner, *The Urge to the Sea: The Course of Russian History—The Role of Rivers, Portages, Ostrogs, Monasteries, and Furs* (Berkeley, Calif.: University of California Press, 1942), p. 34.

[6] Platonov, *Proshloe*, pp. 23–24.

[7] For a brief description of the functions of early bodies of peasant self-government, see Jerome Blum, *Lord and Peasant in Russia from the Ninth to the Nineteenth Century* (Princeton: Princeton University Press, 1961), p. 96.

be higher in keeping with the measure of their satisfaction in handling their own affairs. Along the southern and western shores of the White Sea, where few farmers settled because of the barrenness of the soil, the power of the boyars of Novgorod and their middle-class partners came to predominate. But in southern regions, such as along the banks of the Northern Dvina and the Onega rivers, the peasantry predominated and democratic forms of organization were the rule.[8] Locked in combat with an inhospitable environment that taxed every man's resources, scattered broadly throughout a broad landscape that forced each frontiersman to face manifold dangers often alone, the colonists from Novgorod had no doubt that their institutions should preserve the individualism that their experiences in the wilderness necessitated. The private resourcefulness and individualism of these far-flung communities were also reflected in the entire political and social system of the town that governed the empire in which they lived.

There was yet another feature of life in the Russian north that encouraged democracy. From earliest times the princes of the southern half of the Kievan state customarily employed cavalry as their prime fighting forces in combatting foreign enemies or rival lords. The open steppe, where foes could move with great speed, demanded this reliance upon mounted warriors. Kievan princes also hired Pechenegs, Torks, and other nomadic cavalrymen as mercenaries during civil wars. But the princes of the Russian north usually relied upon infantry as their basic army, frequently hiring Varangians to serve in this capacity. Interestingly, there is no record of foreign cavalry units from the south ever bringing victory to their princes over infantry forces from the north. Varangians and infantry brigades drawn from the populace of Novgorod, for example, achieved victory for Prince Vladimir over Yaropolk. Later Yaroslav's northern foot soldiers won his triumph over Sviatopolk. Yet southern Russian princes continued to rely upon mounted war bands (the *druzhina*) except when massive foreign incursions threatened to overwhelm them. At such times the cavalry were reinforced by town militias of infantry in which peasants also served as conscripts.[9]

[8] Platonov, *Proshloe*, p. 24.

[9] Soloviev, 1: 233. Minor engagements usually were fought by the *druzhina,* which seems to have developed a sense of elitist superiority over the foot soldiers. When infantry were employed in inter-princely feuds, they were used as cannon fodder and shock troops, perhaps because their involvement in internecine fighting did not engender the enthusiasm and martial spirit that were shown at times of true national crisis. See Vernadsky, *Kievan Russia,* p. 192; V. I. Sergeevich, *Drevnosti russkogo prava* (Saint Petersburg, 1908–11), 1:595–618.

Obviously the cavalry forces of the Kievan princes were made up largely of boyars who made military pursuits their main occupation and were far superior to national infantry detachments in their technical expertise and professional training. How can their inferiority to the infantry in battle be explained? William McNeill once suggested that Athenian democracy may have been an accidental result of the ancient Greeks' reliance upon the phalanx as their prime fighting formation. When men are pressed into combat in such close formation that each man's body is partially covered by the shield of his neighbor, the ability of each individual becomes the sole criterion for judging his merit and his personal worth. When a man's safety depends upon the strong right arm of the comrad who wields his sword by his side, feelings of egalitarianism cannot help but arise. In the heat of combat no one would question his neighbor about his origins, his social standing, or his place of birth. The man who showed bravery and skill in killing the enemy and defending the phalanx would emerge as the praiseworthy individual and would gain the respect and estimation of his fellow soldiers. Upon their return to peaceful pursuits, those who had experienced the camaraderie of the phalanx could never favor institutions, laws, or customs that discriminated against men on the basis of anything other than pure ability and personal performance. Thus the democracy of the Greek city-state owed its origins to the natural egalitarianism of the foot soldier and the simple attitude of those who served in the phalanx.[10] Perhaps similar forces were at work in the Russian north. If the democratic institutions of Novgorod were not inspired by the experiences of the town militias, then the spirit of the militias must have been a consequence of the civic pride that enkindled the enthusiasm of the infantry and inflamed their desire to fight well on behalf of their principality. Beyond this cautious conjecture the conscientious historian cannot venture.

While the empire of Novgorod continued its work of colonizing the north, the southern sectors of the Kievan state suffered a series of disasters that sapped their strength and caused political turmoil and economic decline. Southern princes became powerless to restrain the depredations of the Polovtsy, who raided Rus almost at will. Rampant civil disorder, which was expressed in as many as fifty separate civil wars within two centuries, hardened the conditions of life throughout the south. The widespread fighting ruined innumerable small agricultural holdings, forcing free farmers to seek indenture as a means of averting death by

[10]William H. McNeill, *The Rise of the West* (Chicago: University of Chicago Press, 1963), pp. 198–200.

starvation. Powerful landlords took advantage of the squabblings of their princes to conduct their affairs in almost sovereign fashion, all the while ignoring the basic premises of social justice. Indenture and bondage became widespread among the lower social strata, as the turmoil along the steppe made it impossible for independent farmers to survive. The once large class of free farmers declined to insignificance. Warfare and concomitant economic disruption ruined the commercial enterprises of the middle class and thereby occasioned the decline of towns. In the lands of the northeast Russian princes began to devise political theories that disregarded the accountability demanded by the veche and the boyar duma, and created forms of government that were antithetical to the spirit of traditional Kievan society. Only in Novgorod was the social and political order of earlier Kievan times able to survive a bit longer. Everywhere else throughout Rus the satisfactions of a once free existence became a dim memory and a hope for the future.

It is difficult to believe that economic reasons lay solely at the heart of Kievan troubles during the twelfth century. Although the Fourth Crusade had deprived Russian merchants of much of their lucrative trade with Constantinople and the Polovtsy had hampered trade and agricultural growth along the steppe, there were other economic activities that could have compensated for these losses. The riches of the forest zone, animate and inanimate, still remained virtually untapped. Novgorod and Pskov were gathering an increasingly large share of Baltic commerce. Indeed, Novgorod was winning reputation as the fur capital of the civilized world because of its valuable exports. Handicraft production, which was very important to the economy of Kiev and other major economic centers, expanded significantly during the century that preceded the coming of the Mongol hordes.[11]

The notion that the decline of Kiev was due more to the loss of mobility of its populace is more satisfying. The striking increase in the number of indentured farmers in Rus between, say, the years 1050 and 1200 can be attributed to the arrest of Russian frontier expansion by the Polovtsy and other belligerent neighbors. The people of the Kievan south found access to the steppe impossible, unless they wished to risk the virtual certainty of meeting a bad end. Passage northward, to Novgorod and its environs, was barred by impassable forests and bogs. Migration to the northeast was possible and by the mid-twelfth century was well underway. But the pitfalls awaiting these migrants will be examined in the following chapter. The people of Rus found that their horizons had become narrowly circumscribed. Once the Russian peasant was deprived of the safety valve

[11] B. A. Rybakov, *Remeslo drevnei Rusi* (Moscow, 1948), pp. 521–22.

that frontier regions had offered him, he fell easy prey to ambitious landlords and central authorities who wished to subdue him to the needs of the national economy and the state. Throughout the twelfth century a startling increase in the power and privileges of the boyars was evident throughout all Russia, as was the expansion of their landholding and their control of the peasantry.[12] Unable to flee to new locales, the once free farmer found no effective means to oppose the burgeoning might of the landed aristocracy. Thus was begun a process which ended, for additional reasons soon to be seen, not only in the complete disappearance of mobility but in the total loss of all personal freedom.

Even during the last days of the Kievan state, there were those who chose to risk everything upon a headlong and desperate flight to the southern frontier rather than submit to increasingly certain bondage. Russian society was never without such individuals. These adventurers took to the steppe and exposed themselves to constant peril from barbaric roaming enemies. But the vastness of the steppe and the sparseness of its population afforded some hope that they could establish a more rewarding way of life without detection by enemies. Like small ships in an immense sea, individuals and families erected their homesites and appropriated farming land on the prairie or pursued a more nomadic way of life by hunting, fishing, or relying upon robbery for their keep. Although discovery might mean instant death or slavery, the individualism provided by this free existence was compensation enough for those who chose it.

Occasionally these pioneers formed their own communities for mutual assistance and military defense. Among these early forerunners of the cossacks were the so-called *brodniki,* who in the area of the lower Don River established a commune of frontiersmen who recognized neither the power of the prince of Kiev nor that of the Polovtsy. Living by fishing and defending themselves through their ferocity in battle, the *brodniki* kept their community intact until the Mongol invasion. Similar communities seem to have existed on the lower Dniester River and along the lower Danube.[13] But these vagabonds were totally estranged from their former homeland and their activities were all but unknown among those whom they had left. For this reason their democratic spirit and their enterprising activities were unable to have any impact on the Kievan state or to

---

[12] A. E. Presniakov, *The Formation of the Great Russian State,* trans, A. E. Moorhouse (Chicago: Quadrangle Books, 1970), p. 43.

[13] Vernadsky, *Kievan Russia,* pp. 158, 237–38; P. V. Golubovsky, "Pechenegi, Torki i Polovtsy," in Kiev. Universitet; *Izvestiia,* Nov. 1883, pp. 586–604, Dec. 1883, pp. 707–8. Vernadsky suggests that the term *brodniki* originally meant "fishermen" (p. 158). It seems more likely that the word meant "rovers," or "wanderers."

promote any of the features of its political and social life that earlier can be attributed to the influence of the frontier.

During the decline and fall of the Kievan south, which reached its final stage with the Mongol invasion of 1237–40, the empire of Novgorod preserved both its vigorous economic life and its republican institutions. The reasons for Novgorod's continued viability can easily be traced to the frontier life of the principality. The abundant lands of the north still functioned as a safety valve for Novgorod's farmers and enterprisers, while the Hanseatic League offered a new frontier of another nature. The frontier saved the town from the Mongol invasion. When Batu's armies encountered the inhospitable climate and rough terrain in which Novgorod lay, they decided to pursue their fortunes elsewhere. The Mongols had little taste for struggles with nature; the subjection of men was more in keeping with their inclination. So Novgorod was spared the terrible devastation that fell on the other towns of Rus. While Rus lay prostrate under the Mongol yoke, Novgorod preserved Kievan institutions, maintained a sound economic base upon which various Russian princes had to rely from time to time, and functioned as a sanctuary of old Russian culture.

During the dark years that lay ahead, Russians who were mindful of their antecedents in the Kievan state and who mourned its demise kept alive the dream of returning someday to the liberty and opportunity of that frontier society. As Russia suffered through its Dark Ages, bearing humiliation, tribulation, and deprivations of every sort, the vision of that once free society and the men who made it never lost its power to impel later Russians to seek escape to a land where such benefits could again be realized. The spirit that runs through the *Song of Igor's Campaign* and other early Russian writings never lost its power to motivate adventurers to spurn the advantages of civilization for a free but uncertain existence in remote lands. The unknown author of the *Igor Tale* did not realize that he was expressing a sentiment that would become the distinguishing mark of many later settlers on the steppe when he wrote:

> It is far better to be slain
> than to live in slavery;
> so, brothers, let us mount
> our swift stallions
> and have a look at the blue Don.[14]

In later centuries the Russian state would produce many wanderers who wished a similar look at the Don.

[14]A. S. Orlov, *Slovo o Polku Igoreve,* 2d ed. (Moscow-Leningrad, 1946), p. 68.

IV.   The Loss of Frontiers

FEW PEOPLES IN HISTORY have suffered a national disaster as terrifying in its violence, as total in its devastation, and as negative in its effects as the Mongol invasion of Kievan Rus. Operating with deft precision, the armies of Batu Khan reduced much of Rus to ruins and methodically exterminated much of its population. The towns of Kiev and Riazan were scenes of systematic slaughter that claimed virtually the entire citizenry. In other towns, where the Mongols penetrated the town walls and seized the townsfolk, large segments of the population were burned alive in their churches, put to the sword, or killed in torments with a thoroughness the world would not see again until the twentieth century. On the few occasions that Russian princes were able to mount anything that resembled coordinated military opposition, their forces were crushed by overwhelming numbers or cut to pieces by the skill and organization of Mongol commanders. Where the fighting and massacres were most severe, large expanses of Rus became wasteland. Later travelers told of seeing hundreds of bones and skulls scattered about destroyed towns, particularly near Kiev. Important examples of Kievan architecture, libraries, monasteries, and other evidence of the lofty civilization that had radiated from Kiev were no more. Those who survived this holocaust were not consoled by the remembrance that even during the invasion Russian princes had continued to fight each other in civil wars, neglecting the common defense of their homeland for the vain dream of securing personal advancement and gain. Clearly the political history of Kievan Rus had reached its end, as its social disintegration had foretold generations earlier.

The Mongol invasion was as destructive to the Russian economy as the Thirty Years War would later be for the Germans. Even after the initial incursions, when Batu Khan decided to rule the Russian land from his distant capital at Sarai, the steady and calculated ruin of the economy continued. The wealth that had been won by the enterprising commercial work of the Kievan middle class was drained away by Mongol taxes. Ten percent of the young men of Russia, men needed for economic recovery, were recruited for service in the Mongol armies. Many of them were not to see their native land again. The central southern portions of the Kievan state became desolate. Handicrafts and trade of every sort withered. Attempts at recovery were hindered by new Mongol depredations. Between 1237 and 1462 chronicles record some forty-eight major punitive expeditions launched from Sarai against various Russian princes and their subjects for failure to meet continued Mongol demands for revenue and manpower. These raids revisited on the Russian people, albeit on smaller scale, some of the horrors of Batu's invasions of 1237–40. Loss of life and destruction of property created chaotic conditions in which normal economic activity became difficult and at times impossible.[1]

The towns of Rus, many of them battered and some all but extinct, lost their former positions as centers of economic life. Many of the skilled craftsmen who had caused Russian handicrafts and native industry to flourish even until Batu's coming were recruited into the service of Sarai and were resettled in the Golden Horde. The Mongol khans adopted this strategy not only to place the unusual skills of these craftsmen at the service of the Mongol Empire but to deny Russians the use of their expertise. Deprived of those who could produce weapons and design fortifications, the Russian princes experienced a technological lag in armaments and could hardly refuse to comply with the orders that issued from Sarai. But handicraft production in general suffered from this policy. By the end of the first century of the Mongol yoke, the towns of Rus thus lost their principal economic function and further declined in importance.[2] Suzdal, which had prided itself on its skill in church construction, found that its expertise in this area completely vanished during the initial phases of the Mongol domination. When Moscow later attempted to revive Suzdal's architectural work for its own benefit, it discovered that the town preserved no remembrance of its former skills.[3]

Commerce, which had declined during the twelfth century, suffered almost total stagnation throughout the next century. Only in Novgorod, which had escaped the Mongol invasion, was vigorous trade still practiced. The northern overland trade route from the Russian northeast to the kingdom of the Volga Bulgars died out, for the Bulgars had sustained an even more devastating blow from the Mongols than had Rus. Trade between old commercial centers on the Dnieper and the newer towns of the Russian forest zone faltered because of the inability to maintain lines of communication and transportation. Underpopulation and devastation caused southern Pereiaslav to become an economic void. Expansion and colonization to the east terminated from dire necessity, for all the

[1] Joseph T. Fuhrmann, *The Origins of Capitalism in Russia* (Chicago: Quadrangle Books, 1972), pp. 14–15.

[2] Blum, *Lord and Peasant*, p. 63.

[3] Presniakov, p. 61.

resources and energies of those who had survived the Mongol onslaught were required for the day-to-day business of staying alive.[4] At the same time the Russian principalities found themselves isolated from all western trade. From the early thirteenth century the German knights who had taken possession of Livonia barred Russians from access to the Baltic Sea, while the advance of Lithuania stripped from Rus provinces that had been of great economic importance to the Kievan state. Until the seventeenth century many of these territories remained oriented toward central Europe and were lost to other Russian lands as trading partners.[5]

Even before the Mongol invasion it is probable that individuals, small groups, and families from the Kievan south had already resolved to abandon their hazardous surroundings and the faltering economy of the steppe and to strike out in search of a new abode. The safety valve once provided by the steppe was now closed. Hence, this migration wended its way primarily northeastward, into lands of the forest zone that stretched away toward the principality of Vladimir-Suzdal. That the grand prince had already transferred his seat to this region encouraged in these emigrants hope that security and a better livelihood could be found in this direction. After the massacres of Batu, this process of migration was intensified, as many sought to remove themselves from close proximity to the Mongol encampments. The region of the Oka and upper Volga rivers became the new homeland of these refugees from the south.[6] But this was not a flight to a new frontier. The lands into which these settlers poured were set in forest fastnesses that easily isolated a man from contact with the world beyond. The emigrants also encountered native populations of Finns and colonists from the central and southern sectors of Kievan Rus who had colonized these lands in earlier times as a spontaneous process of settlement that had not been directed by princes.[7]

Like pioneers everywhere, the new settlers of the northeast sought to adjust to their new neighbors and the conditions of their new homeland as quickly as possible. They were not assimilated by the native Finns, because the earlier Slavic migrations provided them with local kinsmen and the feeling of participation in a national group that promoted ethnic consciousness and continuity of national values. Their religion, which immediately set them apart from the pagan Finns, also provided a basis for

[4] Ibid.

[5] Philipp, p. 20.

[6] Kliuchevsky, *History*, 1:197–202. Kliuchevsky's arguments for this northeastern migration are often challenged by later historians. This reader finds his proofs as strong and convincing today as his contemporaries believed them to be.

[7] A. V. Ekzempliarsky, *Velikie i udel'nye kniazia severnoi Rusi v tatarskii period s 1238 po 1505 g.* (Saint Petersburg, 1889), 1:1–2.

exclusiveness that preserved self-identity. Like settlers in the United States centuries later, many of these pioneers brought with them to their new land the names of their former settlements in the south and applied them to their new homesites. At times the origins of these migrants can be traced from these relocated names.[8] As the influx from the south continued, the Finnish element found itself without traditions and a self-consciousness powerful enough to maintain its identity and was assimilated by these new neighbors. From this amalgam came the basic stock of the Great Russian people.

Slavs have never been a wandering people. Even when colonizing large areas, such as the Balkan Peninsula during Byzantine times, Slavs have gradually absorbed new regions, settling them thoroughly and assimilating them before advancing farther. Unlike the peoples of the steppe, whose restless energy often carried them from the far reaches of Asia into the heart of central Europe, Slavic peoples have been more restrained in their movements. The migration toward the northeast was a similar type of resettlement. Few of the emigrants probably had the means to undertake a massive journey from the borders of the steppe to the Volga-Oka region. Undoubtedly they made their way into the taiga by careful stages, pausing to work when the opportunity presented itself and acclimitizing themselves to the strange and difficult environment before moving onward. Throughout their journey they probably had to seek temporary employment on the lands of landholders and princes, where they recovered their strength and set aside provisions for the next stages of the migration. Thus even before they encountered the princes of the Volga-Oka region, they had become accustomed to working the lands of others and to hiring out their labor to secure their daily bread. For the regions into which they had penetrated were so thickly forested and overgrown that to clear new land for agriculture would be a long enterprise delaying the refugee in his main task, that of fleeing the danger and destitution that lay behind him.

While those seeking escape from civil disorder, Mongol raids, indenture, and the poor conditions of the south pressed on toward the northeast, emigrants from the empire of Novgorod entered the forest zone for similar reasons. Clashes of aristocratic clans and extortion by wealthy middle-class families who had triumphed over the veche had given the lower classes of Novgorod a taste of some of the misfortunes that had befallen their brethren in other Russian principalities.[9] The

    [8] M. K. Liubavsky, *Obrazovanie osnovnoi gosudarstvennoi territorii velikorusskoi narodnosti; zaselenie i ob"edinenie tsentra* (Leningrad, 1929), pp. 4–16.
    [9] S. F. Platonov, *A History of Russia,* ed. Frank A. Golder, trans. Emmanuel Aronsberg (Bloomington, Ind.: University Prints and Reprints, 1964), p. 79.

Volga-Oka region in all likelihood also experienced an influx of refugees from the upper Volga region. Whenever Tatar punitive expeditions struck the trans-Volga area, they tended to follow the course of the Volga, avoiding the thick forests that bordered it and in which their forces were unable to operate with full efficiency. Seldom did Mongol war bands turn upon tributary rivers. Life along the Volga therefore became perilous, and Mongol havoc devastated the local economies. Discouraged and terrified by these incursions, some of the inhabitants of the upper Volga fled southward toward the more sheltered and secure sanctuaries of the great forests.[10] The territory bounded by the towns of Vladimir, Suzdal, and Moscow found itself therefore at the center of a constricting populace that flowed into its jurisdiction from all points of the compass.

Those who reached the lands of the northeast were probably not disappointed in the new conditions of their life. Refugees who had sought safety from Mongol raids and civil warfare found the region quite peaceful. Between 1293 and the raid of Tokhtamysh that followed Dmitry Donskoi's victory at Kulikovo Pole in 1380, the town of Moscow and its environs were free from any known Mongol violence.[11] Those who sought economic betterment found their new homeland rich in free land and, at least initially, plentiful in meat and forest products. Although the land was heavily wooded and seemed inhospitable to farming, once the timber was felled and burned and its ashes used as natural fertilizer, the soil proved quite suitable for agriculture. The climate, though unpredictable, afforded at least the possibility of regular and bounteous harvests. Those who came to avoid indenture and personal dependence upon landlords and those who dreamed of finding homesteads free from the control of others were less pleased. Most of the newly arrived peasants were totally without means. To strike a new beginning on the land it was necessary to hire oneself as labor to a local landholder or to rent land from owners, paying the master a share of the harvest. Most landholders of the region were unskilled in the management of peasant work forces and seem to have preferred the latter alternative. From the start the immigrant found himself saddled with a debt or bound by obligations that limited his personal initiative and compromised his autonomy.[12]

Most of the newcomers to the northeast settled near the towns of the principality of Vladimir-Suzdal. But these towns were not the agricultural, industrial, and commercial centers that the migrants had known in their former locales, but primarily defensive garrisons. These towns, the construction of which had been the work of local princes, knew little

[10]Sir Bernard Pares, *A History of Russia* (New York: Knopf, 1965), p. 79.
[11]Soloviev, 2:454.
[12]Mavor, 1:46.

of the opportunities for self-enterprise and self-determination that had existed in the northern, central, and southern areas of the Kievan state. Here the princes were all-powerful and in control of the lands and resources of their domains. Most of these princes were self-made men. Most had created their towns from wildernesses that boasted little original population. Slowly these princes had succeeded in clearing the forests, providing arable land, and luring settlers to populate and help in the development of their principalities. Taxes on these settlers enriched the princes and provided capital for the further expansion of their towns. The princes were the directors of all these projects. Small wonder that they regarded the finished products of their labor, the towns and their neighboring farming communities, as their own accomplishment, an inviting oasis among the wilds that settlers could use only for a price.[13] Here princes had little appreciation of the Kievan idea that the boyar class had sovereign rights of its own that balanced princely authority. Here the boyars were servants of the proprietor-prince, tenant landholders who received their lands from the prince and usually retained their holdings only as long as the prince was pleased with the service rendered in compensation for these allocations.[14]

So also did the princes regard the destitute and desperate peasants who appeared before them seeking work and refuge. There was no question that the newcomers should not be subject to the authority of the prince and hold their lands under his general ownership. As S. F. Platonov has said: "It was the princes who had built the cities, constructed the highways and the river crossings. When the settlers arrived in their new homes, they found the prince in full possession, and it was from him that they received the land; to him they paid taxes or 'tribute' for its use; and to him they appealed in moments of danger. The prince was not only the sovereign, but the landlord, who had obtained title to the lands by right of a priority claim, and he could, therefore, dictate the conditions of occupation."[15] Here was not a new frontier, but a world of clearly defined and institutionalized private property. The migrant peasant had little choice but to accept the conditions of his new abode.

The princes of the northeast were not disposed to impose upon the incoming labor force obligations or demands that might cause them to move on to new domains. During the first century and a half of the Mongol domination, Russia was troubled by a persistent problem, the

[13]Kliuchevsky, *History*, 1:252.

[14]See the comments of Michael T. Florinsky, *Russia: A History and an Interpretation* (New York: Macmillan, 1947), 1:45.

[15]Platonov, *History of Russia*, p. 68.

shortage of manpower needed to work the land. These were Russia's Dark Ages. Economic activity was bound up with one basic concern, that of providing enough food to support the land and avert famine. Much of the land that had once borne fruitful harvests was now simple wasteland. Foreign travelers often remarked that vast tracts of Russia resembled nothing so much as a desert.[16] Herein was justified the vision and political astuteness of the princes who enticed or otherwise settled on their lands peasants seeking a better way of life. In those days dense population was a trustworthy measure of the political wisdom and power of any prince. The density of population secured by these princes of the northeast not only ensured their own local authority but laid the foundation for the future strength of the princes of Moscow.

For this reason the princes were careful not to discourage new laborers but actively encouraged their entry into their lands by legislation that seemed highly enlightened to those fleeing the massive indenture and widespread misery of other principalities. Obligations and dues were slight. Personal privileges were great, as long as one did not question the ultimate ownership of the land that was being offered. Military conscription was no longer a concern, for these princes relied upon an aristocratic cavalry of professional servitors. The size of the parcels of land given the immigrants was remarkably great, greater than many had dared to expect. The dreaded raids of the Mongols were precluded by the thickness of the forest that surrounded these communities on all sides. Boyars and other independent landlords, in order to rival the munificence of the princes and win their own share of the newfound labor force, had to resort to similar inducements.[17] Overwhelmed by their good fortune, those who arrived in this unexpected haven failed to realize that all these benefits carried a price, that the prince held on every man a promissory note that someday would come due.

The infusion of this new population and the development of massive agriculture that it occasioned caused Russian economic life in the northeast to flourish. Although some scholars have contended that before the reign of Ivan III landholding was without great profit throughout Russia and usually was not preferred to other occupations, such as service at court and in the army,[18] there seems little doubt that the princes and boyars of

[16]See the account of Josafa Barbaro, quoted in Blum, *Lord and Peasant*, p. 61.

[17]Jerome Blum, "The Rise of Serfdom in Eastern Europe," *American Historical Review*, 62 (1957):818; Boris D. Grekov, *Krest'iane na Rusi s drevneishikh vremen do XVII veka* (Moscow-Leningrad, 1964), pp. 515-25.

[18]See, for example, Richard Hellie, *Enserfment and Military Change in Muscovy* (Chicago: University of Chicago Press, 1971), pp. 26-27. Hellie contends that "owning a relatively free commodity was not profitable" (p. 27).

the Volga-Oka region invested unprecedented large shares of their capital
in land. This caused what one recent writer has termed the "discernible
shift in the former balance between agriculture and commerce."[19] We
need not wonder at the virtual disappearance of foreign and domestic
trade during the first century of Mongol rule. Trade and commerce, it has
already been noted, are identifying characteristics of a frontier society. In
the Russian northeast a new type of society was being born, one that
derived its strength from the land and from the regulated labor of those
who worked it. Upon this new basis the future Russian Empire would be
founded.

The migration to the forest zone brought its own problems. Even
though the principality of Moscow labored diligently to continue the influx
of newcomers to lands of their sovereignty, it soon became obvious that
the natural resources of the region were insufficient to support a large
population. The Moscow area was not as rich in natural wealth as were
other principalities. The soil was generally light and sandy. The Moscow
River was deficient in fish. Wildlife, except for rabbits, was thin and grew
thinner as the inhabitants of the area hunted animals to extinction.
Meadow land and pasture were sparse. The trade that passed along the
Moscow River was slight and could not be taxed heavily enough to compensate for the natural deficiencies of the Moscow region, especially since
the eastern and western terminals of this river trade route remained for a
long time in the hands of rival princes who could protest Muscovite duties
by obstructing Moscow's own trade. The availability of forest products
declined as rapidly as had wildlife, for by the early sixteenth century the
disappointing yield of the soil had caused farmers to clear the forests
about Moscow and convert the land to agricultural use.[20] The princes and
the people of Moscow had little choice but to expand their holdings
through conquest and a new wave of colonization.

But this expansion necessitated the application of new principles to
political and social life. A program of conquest required the prince to
secure the services of many professional military men for important positions in his army. As the expansionist policies of Moscow proved successful and the principality began to absorb all rival lands of the northeast,
Moscow needed many more governmental and military servitors than it
possessed. Endemic economic weakness made it impossible to compensate these servitors in money. Land grants and unprecedented privi-

[19]Fuhrmann, pp. 13–14.
[20]P. I. Liashchenko, *History of the National Economy of Russia,* trans. L. M. Herman
(New York: Macmillan, 1949), p. 179; Liubavsky, p. 38.

leges over the farming populace had to be substituted.[21] The proprietorship of the princes was now shared with the class of military servitors,
who comprised the rapidly growing class of military-service landholders.

With the imperiousness that had become traditional, the Muscovite
prince regulated his service court in its loyalties and responsibilities. Servitors were committed to the service of the prince by service contracts.
Henceforth they could divorce themselves from his service only with his
consent. The grants of service-tenure estates and patrimonies brought the
servitors into almost immediate conflict with the migratory population
that had settled these lands. The service landholders found their peasantry still fluid, eager to pursue freedom and personal advantage from the
estates of one landholder to another when better opportunities presented
themselves. Obligated to render service to his prince no matter how conditions were on his estates, the service landholder was naturally anxious
to still the wanderlust of his peasants and bind them to his own service. A
mobile peasantry threatened the efficiency and reliability of his own
service to the prince.[22] In this manner the notion that the prince was
owner of all land was refined to include the idea that the prince had to be
served by all who settled his lands. As Platonov has noted: "Directly or
indirectly the entire population of the state became subject to the Muscovite sovereign,"[23]

The new measures being implemented at the Muscovite court were,
for the time being, unknown to the peasantry. Their import would become
clear later, when total loss of mobility made it impossible for the
peasantry to escape the finely woven noose of serfdom slowly being drawn
about them. Their gratitude for having been admitted to the serenity and
relative abundance of the Volga-Oka region had prompted the peasants
to accept without question or complaint the principle that the land that
they worked belonged to another and could never become their own personal property. Even when settling untenanted wastelands, the peasant
learned to regard these barren tracts as the property of the prince.[24] But
until the sixteenth century the peasant's personal freedom and his right to
leave his lands remained unquestioned, and with this freedom remained
the hope that some day he could migrate to a still better land and become

[21]Boris Brutzkus, "The Historical Peculiarities of the Social and Economic Development
of Russia," in Class, Status, and Power, ed. Reinhard Bendix and Seymour Lipset (New
York: Free Press, 1953), p. 519.

[22]S. F. Platonov, The Time of Troubles, trans. John T. Alexander (Lawrence: University
of Kansas Press, 1970), pp. 8–12.

[23]Ibid., p. 12.

[24]Mavor, 1:47.

the master of his own acreage. Compared to the incipient indenture that he had fled, his new life seemed a great improvement over what had befallen those who had not migrated to the northeast.

During the fourteenth and fifteenth centuries the citizens of the Muscovite realm began to tread the path that the peoples of western Europe had trod centuries before. In the Russian forest zone settlers were subjected to the immobile way of life and the loss of frontiers that the West had witnessed after the collapse of the Roman Empire. The reason for the similarity between Russian life during this period and that of the West during the early Middle Ages can be found in the pastoral nature of both communities. Unlike the Eastern Roman Empire, the Western Roman Empire had no great municipal centers, save the city of Rome itself. When Rome declined in its power, population, and economic vitality, the entire area that is today western Europe was left without urban centers. Because cities were not only the transmitters of civilization and learning but the principal locations of trade, crafts, and other diverse forms of economic enterprise, these occupations declined with the demise of city life. Deprived of the influences of the city, life throughout the rest of the state became monotonous and undifferentiated. Mobility suffered, for the cities had provided new and diverse activities for those who wished to quit agricultural work. Without the political leadership traditionally provided by municipal centers, the countryside had to create its own political and social institutions. These were designed to protect the agricultural mode of production upon which all life depended. Feudalism and manorialism were the extreme measures that the peoples of the West adopted until the cities were reborn and other forms of economic activity returned.

During the fourteenth and fifteenth centuries Russia passed through a similar stage of development. The Russian northeast, which was now densely settled, had only one city, Rostov, that existed from early times, even before the formation of the Kievan state.[25] Rostov had early become a thriving commercial metropolis by controlling the eastward passage of German woolen goods and imports of Bulgarian wax from the east. Church architects in Rostov acquired stone from the Bulgars of the Kama River and used this material to erect impressive churches. But this thriving vitality was limited to the town of Rostov itself. Throughout the forest lands surrounding Rostov these endeavors went largely unnoticed.[26] The towns that sprang up later in the Russian northeast were

[25] Rostov is mentioned as part of the political patrimony of Rurik and was assigned by Rurik to one of his lieutenants (*Russian Primary Chronicle*, p. 60).

[26] Presniakov, pp. 11, 44 and 46.

not commercial points. Their location seems to have been determined by the quality of nearby farming land and the density of agricultural labor. None was built on an important river or commercial route, as had been the early towns of Kievan Rus. Vladimir and Suzdal were far removed from any major commercial artery. Pereslavl-Zalessky was a considerable distance from the main Volga trade route. Rostov itself lay upon river trade routes of secondary significance, as did Moscow and Tver. Nizhni Novgorod was perhaps an exception, but its founding had been motivated by political concerns in an attempt to cow local Finnish tribes and challenge the hegemony of the Volga Bulgars.[27] All the towns of the northeast, as has already been noted, were designed primarily as defensive garrisons, strongholds where princes could preserve their power and protect the agriculturists who depended upon them. None of these towns was so different in its life, so cosmopolitan in its atmosphere and habits, that it could offer much of an alternative to the agricultural style of life of the neighboring countryside.

Even the trade of the northeast, sparse though it was, was not of a type to encourage popular participation and afford differentiation in occupation and social status. Until the late fifteenth century interregional trade was conducted largely by landlords, particularly monasteries. The primary commercial enterpriser was the Tsar himself, who relied upon selected agents to manage this business in his name.[28] The class of bourgeois merchants that is so important to European history did not emerge in Russia. Without this intervening stratum between the landowners and the peasantry, social mobility was thwarted, free enterprise remained dormant, and the life of the peasant was restricted to the soil.

Changes in the nature of military service also depressed private initiative among the bulk of the population and closed to them another avenue of personal advancement. The infantry militias of the Kievan period were seen no more. Influenced by their two most estimable enemies, the Mongols and the Poles, Russian princes relied upon cavalry units as their main fighting forces. Infantry detachments of peasants and townsfolk saw use only in providing engineering and supply services in the rear and almost never were committed to combat.[29] Later, when full enserfment of the peasant masses made common soldiers unreliable in any military capacity, the princes and their servitors dared not furnish them weapons,

[27] Tikhomirov, pp. 60–64.
[28] Blum, "The Rise of Serfdom in Eastern Europe," p. 835; Jerome Blum, "Prices in Russia in the Sixteenth Century," *Journal of Economic History* 16 (1956):192–94.
[29] Hellie, p. 25; P. A. Geisman, *Kratkii kurs istorii voennago isskustva v srednie i novye veka* (Saint Petersburg, 1893–96), 1:124–28.

lest these arms be turned against those who had provided them.[30] The
lower classes were no longer regarded by the aristocratic elite as
comrades in arms but merely as helots, whose taxes and manual labor
were their contribution to war efforts. The camaraderie and feeling of
joint enterprise that distinguished Kievan military efforts (and which is
portrayed so vividly, even if idealistically, in Sergei Eisenstein's classic
film *Alexander Nevsky*) withered away during early Muscovite times.
With its disappearance also vanished the leveling influence that exposure
to common danger and responsibility for the common good exert upon
any formation or society of men.

Throughout the fourteenth and fifteenth centuries life in the dense
forests of the Russian northeast remained constant and unvaried. The
slaughters and terrors of earlier times were all but forgotten, except on
the few occasions when the declining Mongol Horde was able to muster
its failing strength to deal the ambitious and recalcitrant prince of
Moscow a blow calculated to keep Russia under the vassalage of Sarai.
The daily struggle with the soil, the lack of frontiers, and the decline of
the towns and cosmopolitan centers made the typical Muscovite
sedentary. During the brief summer the Russian peasant was forced to
labor rapidly and with all his vigor to secure sufficient provisions for the
year ahead. During the winter the bitter cold and deep snows trapped him
within his hut, where he sat upon his stove with his family and waited for
the first signs of spring. These conditions of climate and terrain, coupled
with the conscious efforts of landlords to keep him in place, made their
mark upon the personality of the Great Russian peasant.[31] The restlessness and vitality that so marked Kievan times gave way to an immobility
and a stoical dullness that were mirrored in the social uniformity and economic inactivity that distinguish these centuries.

Within this narrow purview individuals could improve their lot only in
minor ways. Peasants who resettled to the monastery lands that sprang
up throughout the northeast, for example, could usually gain new and attractive benefits. Often such settlers were excused from obligations to the
state for periods of three, five, ten or more years and were considered beyond the jurisdiction of local authorities. As laborers for the church they
were excused from the general obligation to contribute to the upkeep (the

[30]Heinrich von Staden, *The Land and Government of Muscovy: A Sixteenth Century Account,* trans. and ed. Thomas Esper (Stanford, Calif.: Stanford University Press, 1967), p.
88. Von Staden observed that the "Grand Prince cannot get reinforcements except by forcing his peasants into military service; but they are not armed, as are the peasants in the
Christian world, and they know nothing about war" (p. 88).

[31]See the famous description of the character of the Great Russian people by
Kliuchevsky, *History,* 1:218–20.

so-called *kormlenie,* or "feeding") of local officials. Their taxes were often smaller and were collected in the name of the state by monastic tax-gatherers, who were preferable to others performing this service for the government.[32] But these were quantitative improvements. Great qualitative amelioration of living conditions or bold new ventures into new avenues of enterprise and endeavor were totally lacking.

Like the peasant communes of medieval Europe centuries before, the rural inhabitants of the rapidly emerging principality of Moscow followed primitive methods to achieve fundamental objectives. Hemmed in by enemies, exposed to an extreme climate, supported by relatively unproductive soil, caught up in an inert isolationism that stifled all self-expression, the lands of the northeast kept alive Russian national self-consciousness during a period when this consciousness, like that of the Polovtsy or the Volga Bulgars, might have vanished from history. But this victory was bought at a great price. The loss of frontiers between the Mongol invasion and the reopening of the southern and eastern border-lands created a dichotomy between the landlords, who directed the agricultural and commercial work, and the peasants, who "drew their burden" and knew little beyond their own labor. Deprived of a significant middle class, all of Russian society became narrowly constricted. The varied class structure that had accorded Kiev much of its variety and opportunity was replaced by strict cleavage between those who held the land in service tenure and those who supported state servitors through agricultural work. Social mobility vanished. It required merely administrative measures to curtail mobility of any sort. The Muscovite political leadership, which had early acquired a taste for collective obedience to centralized authorities and the subjection of individuals to the grand purposes of the state, was not slow to introduce such measures.

The growth of the principality of Moscow was in reality a reaction to frontier forces. The government of Moscow had one basic feeling toward the frontier lands that fringed its principality: a deep and ingrained fear. The earlier raids of the Pechenegs, Polovtsy and other nomadic tribes had instilled in Russia a dread of the vast spaces that stretched away to the populous lands of Asia. The Mongol invasion, however, brought a horror to Russia that centuries of time could not erase. That disastrous event taught Russian leaders a fundamental lesson they were not to forget when they found themselves once again in control of power and resources sufficient enough to allow them to determine their own affairs: If the Russian land were to survive, the lands that lay beyond its borders had to

[32]Liubavsky, p. 29.

be conquered, subdued, divested of their primitive energy, and made to correspond to Russian institutionalized life. To achieve this end, the Muscovite prince had to bend the will of every subject to the task of supporting the large military forces and the sizeable apparatus of state government this undertaking demanded. In pursuing this aim, the traditional proprietorship of the prince grew to complete despotism, while the sedentary life of the peasant was transformed into a system of complete enserfment. The needs of the state became paramount; the aspirations of its people were subordinated to the designs of the ruling powers. In this process the national institutions of the Russian Empire were created.

V.   The Revival of the Frontier Spirit amid the Foils of Serfdom

BY THE END of the fifteenth century the colonizing movements and migrations of the Russian people had completely halted. To the north of Muscovy migrants seeking more rewarding lands were prevented from farther wandering by the bogs and forests of the Pomorie. In the east volatile and savage tribes, such as the Cheremiss and the Mordvinians, waged constant warfare among themselves and against neighboring Russian territory, making expansion in this direction foolhardy. The west was blocked by the Poles, Lithuanians, and Livonians who, thwarted in their earlier attempts to gain Russian territory, availed themselves of any opportunity to intrude violently into Russian affairs. To the south and southeast lay the lands of the Mongols which, though fragmented by domestic turmoil, still posed a serious threat to the life and property of those who wandered within their spheres of influence. As long as the Russian population had retained at least the possibility of migrating to new homesites, their control and organization had been more difficult for princes and boyars. But during the sixteenth century the Russian princes found for the first time that all hope of relocation was denied their subjects and the populace seemingly could be enlisted in the pursuit of objectives favorable to the interests of the great landowners.[1]

It is hardly accidental that this period also stands as a turning point in Russia's relations with the East. In the reign of Ivan the Terrible Russia launched its mission of subjugating and colonizing the immediate frontier lands from which it had suffered centuries of misfortune. Thus was begun a grand design that eventually carried the banners of the Muscovite state to the shores of the Pacific Ocean and won for Russia an immense territory encompassing one-sixth the entire land area of the globe. Such a plan of massive conquest could not have been undertaken earlier. Then Russia's military might was weaker and its population still fluid and volatile. Foreign involvement of such magnitude could have led to domestic turmoil, problems in the economic sector of the state, and new migrations to the lands being acquired from neighbors. But by the 1550s, when

---

[1]S. F. Platonov, *Ivan the Terrible,* ed. and trans. Joseph L. Wieczynski (Gulf Breeze, Fl.: Academic International Press, 1974), pp. 17–19.

Ivan initiated his campaigns of conquest against the Mongol khanates of Kazan and Astrakhan, the Russian peasant had been securely locked into his occupation and, for all intents and purposes, to the soil which he worked. Ivan's government felt confident that it could restrict peasant mobility and ensure that new safety valves would not upset conditions in the heartlands of the Russian state. The seeds planted by the Russian princes of the northeast had now borne their fruit. Generations of farmers who had accepted the principle that their land was the property of those from whom they had received its use had bequeathed to their descendants a socioeconomic system that could easily be steered into a program of full enserfment of the agricultural strata. By the time of Ivan the Terrible's death in 1584, de facto enserfment had been instituted, even without formal pronouncements to this effect.

But the government of Ivan IV failed to consider one very important factor. Serfdom in Russia was an active and deliberate program sanctioned by landowners to restrain farmers who had once been free and who remembered this freedom. In the West serfdom had appeared as an extension of traditional slavery, based upon the *mansi serviles* and the colonate of the later Roman Empire.[2] In Russia, however, serfdom was imposed, not upon slaves, but upon freemen who traced their independence back to the class of free farmers in Kievan society. For this reason serfdom was not easily maintained in Russia. The implementation of serfdom awakened in the Russian peasant those feelings of independence and personal enterprise, democracy, and individualism, that had been dormant since the decline of Kiev. The Muscovite government, mistaking the acquiescence of the peasant during the fourteenth and fifteenth centuries for indifference toward the loss of personal liberty, was unprepared for the reaction that followed. Throughout the reign of Ivan the Terrible the peasant seized any opportunity to flee his lands and to escape to the wild and unsupervised frontier territories newly opened for colonization by Ivan's victories over the Mongol khanates. Any sort of natural disaster or other national calamity also triggered spontaneous peasant migrations to the east and south. Ivan's Oprichnina, his Livonian war, incursions of the khan of the Crimea, plagues, famines, flood, and drought—all impelled the peasant to seek freedom in remote lands while the government, preoccupied with other matters, was unable to arrest his flight.

The turmoil and excesses witnessed during Ivan's reign caused the

[2]George Vernadsky, "Serfdom in Russia," *Relazione del X Congresso Internazionale di Scienze Storiche,* 3 (Sept. 1955): 249–50.

government temporarily to lose control of the peasantry. Ivan's conquests of Kazan and Astrakhan, though they marked the first great success in Moscow's new aggressiveness against its eastern neighbors, undermined the constraints recently imposed upon the agricultural workers and offered them new mobility. By pacifying the eastern and southeastern borderlands of the Muscovite state, the government ensured the modicum of law and order that made it possible for independent colonists to survive there. A new migration of peasants and runaway bondmen from the center of the Muscovite state to the so-called Lower Reaches along the Volga River and to the steppe south of the town of Tula began and gained in intensity. This flight to the frontier became so massive in its numbers that the economy of the important central provinces of Muscovy was severely disrupted. At one point in Ivan's reign it was estimated that about two-thirds of the arable land in the Moscow district was left fallow, because of a shortage of farmers. Some regions, which had once been rich agricultural centers, were described as wastelands.[3] Those who shunned this migration and chose to remain in place were forced to shoulder additional burdens of taxation in compensation for those who had departed. Consequently, unrest spread and became so great by the closing years of Ivan's administration that the peasants who remained on their lands began to erupt in acts of violence to protest the misery and hopelessness of their situation. Peasants joined common bandits in attacking noble estates and even monasteries in their quest for food, booty, and revenge.[4]

It is quite likely that the peasant flight during Ivan's reign (an exodus that continued well into the next century) greatly facilitated the implementation of serfdom in the central provinces of the state. The economic void created by this migration raised such severe domestic problems that countermeasures by the government became inevitable. There is yet another important consideration. Those who fled were probably the more adventurous, self-reliant, and recalcitrant of the rural populace. Frontier lands have always appealed to the bold and daring, while repelling the weak and the indecisive. Although the presence of so many malcontents on the frontier created a mass of combustible material that later flared repeatedly into conflagrations at any suitable pretext, the absence of these elements from the center of the state allowed the Muscovite government to work its will all the more easily upon the more docile seg-

---

[3]Platonov, *Ivan the Terrible*, p. 117.
[4]V. I. Koretsky, "Iz istorii krest'ianskoi voiny v Rossii nachala XVII veka, *Voprosy istorii*, 1959, no. 3, pp. 120–22.

ments of society that remained. By their flight, discontented peasants may have encouraged the more rapid development of serfdom at home.[5] Occasionally one hears the thesis that Scandinavia today is pacifistic, socialistic, and isolationist because its more dynamic and aggressive elements departed the Scandinavian countries during the Norse exodus into Europe, leaving behind a population that was more tractable. If this argument has any validity, it applies equally well to sixteenth-century Russia. Here the frontier provided the impetus toward the greater centralization and increased authoritarianism that was stated as a corrolary in chapter 1 of this work.

The free existence of the refugees on the steppe and the Lower Reaches proved short-lived. The dislocation that their departure had created among the laboring forces of the state occasioned new pieces of legislation that prevented others from reinforcing their new communities. At the same time the Muscovite government undertook operations to reclaim the laborers and potential taxpayers who lived beyond the reach of Muscovite authorities. Toward the end of his life, Ivan IV resolved to reincorporate these renegades into the state by extending the Russian border farther into the steppe through a series of fortified and interdependent garrison towns. Such outposts would simultaneously guard against invasions by the forces of the Crimean khan (who now became Muscovy's sole but formidable enemy in the south) and bind Russian homesteaders to state service anew. Muscovite commanders and servitors were sent to the steppe to determine the location of free homesteaders, enlist them in the task of building the garrison town, then impress them into service for the defense of the new town to be built in their area. Local inhabitants would receive from the Tsar confirmation of their right to maintain ownership of the lands they had settled. But they would also be required to farm a specified tract of land for the state. The government would provide tools and work animals for this purpose, but the peasant was to farm this plot of state land without compensation. The grain thus produced would supply the aristocratic military servitors of the garrison, relieve shortages rampant throughout the central districts of Muscovy, and often would be sent to similar garrisons farther into the steppe, where agriculture had not yet been instituted. Through this process the free residents found themselves part of the service class of the new town. Although serfdom was not yet extended to these borderlands,

[5]I. G. Rozner, "Antifeodal'nye gosudarstvennye obrazovaniia v Rossii i na Ukraine v XVI-XVIII vv.," *Voprosy istorii*, 1970, no. 8, p. 56.

each inhabitant of the town found himself recommitted to the service obligation he had fled.[6]

In extending their control farther along the steppe, the Muscovite authorities adopted a method that had been used by other sovereigns of Europe to subdue marauders along their borders. Henry the Fowler, for example, had used a similar system in pacifying his eastern borderlands that were ravaged by the raids of the Magyars. Once two garrison towns have been constructed in hostile territory, a line of military operations can be mounted between them that will discourage enemy incursions into that sector. But when a third such town is founded to form a triangle with the first two, the territory within the bounds of that triangle becomes a pacified zone, for enemy operations cannot feasibly be conducted therein. In this instance the Russian government constructed such a system of pacification, not primarily against a foreign invader, but against its own citizens. Resumption of control over subjects, not defense against aliens, seems to have been the primary goal of the government. Finding themselves, in Platonov's phrase, "surrounded with forts," the Russian frontiersmen became entangled anew in the nets of the expanding Muscovite political and social system.[7]

During the brief period of time that these settlers on the steppe and the Lower Reaches had enjoyed their new freedoms, their way of life had not influenced the institutional life of central Russia, except in the negative ways already indicated. Their free style of life and the spirit of individualism and personal liberty that they practiced in their new environs remained peculiar to their own communities and were not in any way reflected in the society they had abandoned. For the Muscovite government had now achieved the power to preserve existing social and economic forms and to fend off influences threatening the established order. One might flee the system temporarily, but one could not change it from within or from without. Thus the frontier characteristics that were prevalent during Kievan times could not penetrate the forests of Muscovy. By the end of the sixteenth century the lands of the Russian northeast became enserfed beneath a system of autocratic rule that now did not hesitate to state its direct proclamations in pretensions to absolute power.

In the Russian north, amid the extensive empire of Novgorod, social and economic conditions had also worsened for the individual, just as the free political life of the principality had vanished after the absorption of Novgorod by Moscow during the reign of Ivan III. Novgorod had proved

[6]Platonov, *Ivan the Terrible,* pp. 123–24; Platonov, *Time of Troubles,* pp. 38–39.
[7]Platonov, *Time of Troubles,* p. 71.

most difficult for Moscow to bend to its will. As the expansion of Moscow
had continued apace at the expense of its neighbors, Novgorod's peculiar
geographical position and vibrant spirit of independence had afforded the
hope that the town could escape incorporation into the Muscovite system.
In Moscow tens of thousands of military servitors had to be provisioned
and maintained for service on estates throughout the principality. This
circumstance alone ensured that the land and its farmers would be
recruited to support this armed force; therefore serfdom or something
similar was almost a necessity in the forest zone. But the Russian north
was unaffected by such considerations. Military service estates were rare
in the north, for the land was too barren to support such reserves.
Cavalry units, the fundamental fighting units of the princes of Moscow,
were not maintained for the defense of the north, because the enemies of
Novgorod, such as the Swedes, attacked in boats from the sea and along
the rivers or else mounted sudden strikes from the forests and swamps,
where horsemen were at a great disadvantage. The peasant labor of the
north consequently was free from the constraint and control associated
with the obligation of supporting military reserves and continued to function according to the principles of the *mir,* the *volost,* and other local
agencies of autonomous self-government.[8]

For these reasons the independence and spirit of adventure that
marked the society of Novgorod from ancient times continued to manifest
themselves throughout the period of the Mongol yoke. At times the
boundless energies of the Novgorodians could not be contained even by
the vast empire they administered and spilled over to complicate Muscovite affairs. At such times Muscovite officials experienced something of
the frontier spirit that they had subdued so successfully in their own
domains. Bands of freebooters from Novgorod, who are known in the
chronicles as the "boatmen" (*ushkuiniki*), bored with their lot at home,
often took to the river systems of central Russia and, much like their
Norse predecessors, sought adventure and gain wherever they could be
found. Their operations were so organized and well provisioned that the
suspicion remains that they were financed in their raids by wealthy
merchant families of Novgorod, who hoped to derive profit from their ex-
ploits.[9] In 1375 the Voskresensk Chronicle reports that some seventy
boatloads of these "brave lads" (as they were often known in Novgorod)
attacked and sacked the town of Kostroma and took captive many men,

[8]Platonov, *Proshloe,* pp. 66–68.
[9]George V. Lantzeff and Richard A. Pierce, *East to Empire: Exploration and Conquest on
the Russian Open Frontier to 1750* (Montreal: McGill-Queen's University Press, 1973),
p. 36.

women, and children, whom they sold into slavery among the Bulgars of the Volga. They defeated a large Muscovite army near Kostroma, then burned and pillaged the town of Nizhni Novogrod. Their insatiable desire for adventure drove them to the southern Volga, where they were finally massacred by Moslem authorities near the town of Astrakhan. "The Moslems seized all their wealth," Russian chroniclers remarked with relief of their fellow Christians, "and so perished these evil brigands."[10] Before their destruction at Astrakhan they had demonstrated to Moscow the initiative and enterprise that Novgorod could still muster, for between 1360 and 1375 the "brave lads" had at various times pillaged Kostroma, Viatka, Yaroslavl, and other towns along the rivers of central Russia.[11]

But during the fifteenth and sixteenth centuries Novgorod declined in influence, population, and vitality for a number of reasons. The Hanseatic League, which had brought the principality much of its wealth, had seen its day. Moscow's growing military might had begun to alarm Russia's western neighbors to such an extent that the commercial towns of Livonia imposed a virtual embargo on trade with Novgorod, lest imported technical innovations and specialists in military matters find their way to Moscow and strengthen its military capability. At the same time Moscow acquired new and more profitable trade routes with the English and the Dutch through the White Sea, depriving Novgorod of its role of commercial middleman between the forest zone and the West. The loss of commercial business, coupled with the resettlements of population made by Ivan III and the terrible purge that Ivan IV inflicted on the town, caused the population of Novgorod to decline markedly. Between 1546 and 1582 Novgorod experienced a decline in population from 5,000 families to about 1,000, leading one modern historian to remark that "the entire territory of Novgorod was turned into a desert."[12] The decline of economic opportunity was reflected in social disruption. Conditions throughout society worsened because of the growing power of the aristocracy and the middle class. As early as the 1420s a birchbark letter testifies to the flight of Novgorodian peasants from their lands because of excessive demands made upon their labor and excessive taxes levied upon them.[13] The economic and social disintegration of Novgorod made it an easy victim of the centralized and well-managed power of the princes of Moscow.

[10] Arkheograficheskaia komissiia, *Polnoe sobranie russkikh letopisei* (Saint Petersburg: 1841–), 8, cols. 23–34.

[11] Lantzeff and Pierce, pp. 36–37.

[12] Platonov, *Time of Troubles,* pp. 31–32.

[13] R. E. F. Smith, *The Enserfment of the Russian Peasantry* (Cambridge: Cambridge University Press, 1968), p. 53.

Novgorod's love for adventure and willingness to pursue the possibility of an unregulated way of life were seemingly not without influence upon later Russian history. Something of the spirit of Novgorod seems to have been carried by its emigrants and exiles to new frontier regions, where the individualistic traits of Novgorod lived on and colored the attitudes of others who shared its loathing of the rigid political and social system being developed by Moscow. When Ivan III subjugated Novgorod, he relocated some eight thousand of its leading citizens to new homesites. It is significant, however, that in this instance Ivan did not follow the usual Muscovite custom of deporting such exiles to frontier lands but ordered them resettled in Vladimir, Pereiaslavl, Yuriev, and other provinces nearer Moscow. Apparently the well-known spirit of insurrection of Novgorod demanded that these potential rebels be kept closer within the reach of Muscovite authorities.[14] But these exiles do not seem to have remained long in their appointed new abodes but drifted toward freer lands. Customs, dress, and dialects easily identifiable as of Novgorodian origin can be found among the later Russian inhabitants of Siberia.[15] It is also possible, as some scholars have recently suggested, that the famed democracy and love of freedom of the cossack communities were imported to the steppe from Novgorod, Pskov, and other northern towns, where political life had been strongly determined by the rule of the veche.[16] Unable to counter the supremacy of the Muscovite state system, these remnants of the old Kievan frontier society apparently found new expression and exerted new influences along the borderlands of the Russian Empire, where struggles against the forces of nature and wild enemies offered a much greater hope for personal development and an individualized existence than did further opposition to the growing power of Moscow and its satraps.

The Muscovite policy of "removal" (*vyvod*), which presaged the later practice of placing politically unreliable elements under administrative exile in areas at great distances from the center of Russian life, also contributed to the accumulation of potentially dangerous elements along the Russian frontiers. During the reign of Ivan IV the Holy Roman Emperor voiced fears that some nine thousand prisoners taken by Muscovite armies during Ivan's Livonian war had been sold into slavery. The em-

[14]V. O. Kliuchevsky, *Istoriia soslovii Rossii,* 3d ed. (Petrograd, 1918), pp. 150–51; V. N. Bernadsky, *Novgorod i novgorodskaia zemlia v XV veke* (Moscow-Leningrad, 1961), pp. 320–22.

[15]L. V. Cherepnin, "Istoricheskie usloviia formirovaniia russkoi narodnosti do kontsa XV v.," in Akademiia nauk SSSR, *Voprosy formirovanii russkoi narodnosti i natsii: Sbornik statei* (Moscow-Leningrad, 1958), p. 133.

[16]See, for example, I. F. Bydakorov, *Istoriia kazachestva* (Prague, 1930), p. 112.

peror was relieved to learn that all had been resettled in various frontier towns by the Tsar. Probably out of fear that the Catholic and Protestant views of these captives would challenge the Orthodoxy of his subjects, Ivan had them stationed along his borders, where their personal attitudes would not undermine Russian religious exclusiveness and where their military skills could be used to good advantage by their captors. Russian sources of the same time report the presence of an additional 150 foreign prisoners of war in the garrison town of Laishevo on the Kama River. These captives helped Russian forces defend the approaches to Kazan against Siberian tribesmen by controlling the fords that crossed the Kama. They also engaged in agriculture on lands alloted them by the Muscovite state. After the conclusion of the Livonian war most of these prisoners seem to have spurned repatriation, preferring to remain in their new surroundings, which they apparently found more attractive than life in their former homelands.[17]

After Ivan IV conquered Kazan and Astrakhan, the Russian government encouraged Russian peasants to populate the lands of Nizhgorod, Arzamas, and Murom in order to augment the Russian population of the middle Volga borderlands. Peasants and others wishing a new way of life seem to have taken quick advantage of this opportunity to seek new and freer horizons. The area of the middle Volga also served Ivan as a place of exile for boyars and other servitors who had fallen into disgrace and disfavor or who had been torn from their patrimonies by the policies of the Oprichnina.[18] These unwilling settlers brought to the frontier their own grudges against Moscow and their considerable skills in military matters and politics. Later many of them would play prominent roles during the violent outbursts of the frontier inhabitants against the Muscovite state.

If our theory concerning the influence of the frontier upon the spirit and institutions of borderlands is true, we would expect to find traces of this influence in the various principalities that bordered the heartlands of the Muscovite state. Many of these principalities had preserved their independence from Moscow as long as Novgorod had and, because of their exposure to wastelands and sparsely inhabited regions, should exhibit the impress of frontier conditions. Although sources for the study of most of these principalities are sparse, extant material seems to affirm the impact of the frontier upon these peripheral territories.

While the principality of Moscow was consolidating its centralized power during the fourteenth and fifteenth centuries, the principality of

---

[17]S. F. Platonov, *Moscow and the West*, ed. and trans. Joseph L. Wieczynski (Hattiesburg, Miss.: Academic International Press, 1972), p. 15.

[18]S. B. Veselovsky, *Issledovaniia po istorii oprichniny* (Moscow, 1963), pp. 149–50.

Riazan was following a different course of evolution. Russia's southern frontier was not clearly delineated from the domains of the Golden Horde. The people of Riazan therefore undertook the gradual colonization of lands that could be removed surreptitiously from Tatar hegemony. Colonists from Riazan moved along the southern courses of the Voronezh and Great Vorona rivers, risking the constant danger of Mongol reprisals. Because of the dangers that attended this activity and the many military alarms to which the men of Riazan were constantly subject, it is hardly surprising that princely power in Riazan was weak and was limited by the desires of the populace to have in their prince one who was primarily a military commander of proven ability.[19] The attitude of the people of Riazan to all higher authority was frequently tinged with disrespect. When the grand prince of Russia had resided in the town of Vladimir, the people of Vladimir had already experienced irreverence and abusive speech directed toward their prince from Riazan. Chronicles report that when addressing the grand prince, inhabitants of Riazan did not shy away from "violent words, according to their custom and their unruliness."[20]

The town of Pronsk was the stronghold of the principality of Riazan in the south, where the colonizing movement had usurped the power of the Mongols and created a new frontier society. Because of the constant perils and pressures to which Pronsk was exposed, the population of the town learned to be alert, enterprising, self-sufficient, and well aware of its abilities. It is hardly surprising that Pronsk soon became totally independent of the town of Riazan and, with its immediate hinterland, became a separate principality.[21] In Pronsk the power of the prince was even slighter than that of the prince of Riazan. The townspeople regulated the tenure of the prince (a circumstance that would seem to indicate the existence of a strong veche) and even refused to allow the prince to interfere in domestic affairs.[22] Although historical materials for the study of Pronsk and Riazan are few, it seems certain that the citizenry of both towns were resourceful, enterprising, and little inclined to submit to patriarchal authority. The earliest cossacks seem to have originated in the principality of Riazan. In 1444 "cossacks" from Riazan are mentioned among the forces that helped defend the town against a Mongol raid,[23]

[19]Presniakov, pp. 104–5, 188–89 and 190.
[20]Tikhomirov, p. 455.
[21]Presniakov, p. 190.
[22]Tikhomirov, p. 459.
[23]V. O. Kliuchevsky, *A Course in Russian History: The Seventeenth Century,* trans. Natalie Duddington (Chicago: Quadrangle Books, 1968), p. 111 (hereafter cited as Kliuchevsky, *Seventeenth Century*).

while many of the Don Cossacks, who are first mentioned in 1502, seem to have been fugitives from Riazan and Pronsk.[24]

The town of Viatka was another frontier outpost that showed little respect for the authoritarian system of the princes of Moscow. Originally founded as a colony of Novgorod (a fact that in itself did much to predetermine much of its later development), Viatka quickly engendered the spirit of insurrection for which its prototype was famed and achieved complete political independence by the end of the twelfth century.[25] During early Muscovite times the people of the principality of Viatka were known as freebooters and wild folk who thrived on piracy and other acts of violence. Viatka frequently raided against its mother city of Novgorod, then struck alliance with Novgorod to obtain assistance from that source in more daring ventures against the towns of the khanate of Kazan, which included the plundering of settlements and the robbing of merchants along the Volga.[26]

The city of Viatka, which was also known as Khlynov, was patterned in its political life upon that of Novgorod and Pskov, but to a more extreme degree. Viatka was ruled by a veche but did not retain a prince even as a figurehead, something that even Novgorod and Pskov had been careful to do.[27] Interestingly, until the sixteenth century the Viatkians allowed no monastery within their territorial limits, perhaps out of fear of the power of monastic communities, which always attempted to encourage agricultural work and more productive and sedate occupations among their neighbors.[28] Agriculture, the Viatkians seemed to understand, was an area of endeavor that exposed one immediately to the possibility of eventual enserfment and the responsibilities of the service state. Like the cossacks, the men of Viatka preferred to forego farming and its attendant risks of regimentation in favor of a mode of production based upon hunting, trapping, and less sedentary enterprises. Writing early in the sixteenth century, Sigmund von Herberstein observed that the inhabitants of Viatka "live without houses and are all, men and women, quick and nimble on their feet and masterly archers, the bow leaving their hands but rarely. They do not give food to their older children, who satisfy themselves from their own shooting."[29] With their interest in plundering

[24] P. N. Miliukov, *Ocherki po istorii russkoi kul'tury* (Saint Petersburg, 1900), 1, pt. 2: 162–63.

[25] N. I. Kostomarov, *Severnorusskie narodopravstva* (Saint Petersburg, 1863), 1: 241–42.

[26] Liubavsky, p. 103.

[27] J. L. I. Fennell, *Ivan the Great of Moscow* (London: St. Martin's Press, 1963), p. 7.

[28] Kliuchevsky, *History*, 2: 162.

[29] Sigmund von Herberstein, *Description of Moscow and Muscovy, 1557*, ed. Bertold Picard, trans. J. B. C. Grundy (New York: Barnes and Noble, 1966), p. 37.

expeditions and their disdain of more pacific economic pursuits, the Viatkians were poor subjects indeed for the authority of landlords and the
ministrations of central officials of government.

By the mid-fifteenth century the various political units of Russia were
subject to the political sovereignty either of Lithuania-Poland or of the
Golden Horde. The Commonwealth of Viatka (as its citizens liked to style
their political entity) was obedient to neither. Nominally within the sphere
of influence of Moscow and thereby loosely answerable to the edicts of
Sarai, Viatka preserved an autonomous but difficult independence until
the power of Moscow grew too great to oppose.[30] As the Golden Horde
declined and disintegrated, leaving Moscow supreme in the forest zone,
Viatka sought to forestall political absorption by playing off Moscow
against Kazan. In 1468 the Viatkians refused to assist Muscovite troops
in a campaign against Kazan, thereby winning Mongol favor. But when
Ivan III asked Viatka for auxiliaries to support his campaign against
Novgorod, Viatka responded with the requested units.[31] This game could
continue only until Moscow was able to devote full attention to the task of
incorporating the commonwealth. In 1489 the metropolitan of Moscow,
who was ever a servant of Muscovite political ambitions, demanded that
Viatka pledge thereafter not to assist the Mongols against the prince of
Moscow. When the metropolitan's ultimatum was answered with silence,
Muscovite troops surrounded the town of Viatka and forced its surrender. Thousands of its citizens were relocated to Moscow and were replaced by more obedient and reliable Muscovite servitors. But even in
defeat Moscow could appreciate the dynamic spirit of the Viatkians.
Many of the relocated men of Viatka were given service-tenure estates
and were recruited into the Muscovite armed forces, where their daring
and resourcefulness could be used to good advantage.[32]

Similar observations of the frontier attitude and institutions could be
made concerning Ustiug, Murom, and other towns that lay along the
boundary of Moscow's sphere of influence. In the end, however, all these
frontier regions met the same fate. The systematic Muscovite order and
its able administrators brought all principalities and commonwealths
under the sway of strong centralized rule and removed the last vestiges of
political and social differentiation throughout the Russian lands. Those
who wished to continue a life on the frontier could do so only by quitting
the Muscovite realm and retreating to sparsely settled and poorly con-

[30]Kliuchevsky, History, 2: 2,4.
[31]Kostomarov, 1: 248–49; George Vernadsky, Russia at the Dawn of the Modern Age
(New Haven: Yale University Press, 1959), p. 100.
[32]Vernadsky, Russia at the Dawn, pp. 100–101.

trolled areas where the heavy hand of Moscow had not yet secured a firm hold. Riazan and Viatka fell because of the political collapse of the Golden Horde. Left with no serious rival in the northeast, the prince of Moscow found it simple to subdue the rebels against his authority, who were now left with no strong power to support them. Moscow's sole great rival, except for the Polish-Lithuanian Commonwealth in the west, was the khan of the Crimea along the southern steppe. Between the lands of the khan and the territories under the sway of Moscow lay a no-man's-land where the authority of both competitors was weak and where daring individuals could seek a new and unrestricted beginning. The next wave of refugees from the Muscovite state accordingly wended its way in this direction.

VI.   The Southern Borderlands

ALONG THE SOUTHERN STEPPE, amid territories contested by the Russians, Poles, and Crimean Tatars, beyond the series of fortresses erected by Ivan the Terrible, refugees from serfdom and despotism were able to bind together in free communities and to preserve their independence by military defense. Like the *brodniki* of Kievan Rus, the cossacks of the south were dauntless frontiersmen who elected to risk their lives in quest of personal liberty by settling lands that still lacked any rule of law. Unlike the malcontents who fled southward in Ivan IV's day, however, the cossacks realized that the individual homesteader could not long preserve his independence from the Muscovite state. Strong military organization and aggressive policies of self-preservation were the means selected by the cossacks to guarantee their continued autonomy.

The formation of the cossack hosts raised for the Muscovite government once again the question of how to extend the borders of the Russian state without encouraging mass migrations to frontier lands. If Muscovite troops followed in the wake of the cossacks and imposed military control over the areas that lay in their rear, the newly pacified zone immediately served as a new safety valve for the release of hundreds, if not thousands, of peasants from their enserfed condition. In 1590, almost a generation after the plans of Ivan IV to reincorporate the southern borderlands into the Muscovite domain had been fulfilled, the Englishman Giles Fletcher testified to the failure of this plan to halt peasant resettlement by observing that throughout Russia "villages and towns stand all unhabited: the people being fled all into other places by reason of the extreme usage and extractions done upon them."[1] Thus the cossacks benefited from the Muscovite feat of occasioning new dislocations among the peasantry as much as they did from the presence of the forces of the Crimean khan as an opponent of further Muscovite expansion southward.

For this reason, Moscow chose to ignore the cossack communities that arose along its southern flank or strove, however possible, to extract political and military gain from these free settlements. Settling in an area where incursions by the Crimeans necessitated strong Muscovite

---

[1] Giles Fletcher, *Of the Russe Common Wealth* (London, 1591), p. 46.

defenses, the cossacks could be used as an unofficial border guard to hinder movements of the armies of the khan, hold the Muscovite border, and sometimes advance it. The earliest cossacks were also employed by various Russian princes and officials on occasion to escort ambassadors and important merchants across the steppe.[2] Cossack war bands also hired themselves out to the Muscovite state as mercenaries when the price was right and at times greatly served Moscow's objectives in this capacity. When official commissions were lacking, the cossacks had few scruples about turning against their onetime employers, raiding their territory, robbing their merchants and even their envoys, and stealing whatever came within their reach.

Inasmuch as the southern frontier lands also adjoined the Caspian region, where commerce with foreign parts was still brisk and profitable, cossacks and the runaway bondmen and peasants who frequently joined their company could also operate within more legitimate businesses and still satisfy their thirst for self-enterprise. During the sixteenth century the town of Astrakhan on the Caspian Sea was a vital commercial center conducting trading operations toward the east that seem to have been even more profitable than the Muscovite trade with Europe that emanated from Archangel and other points on the White Sea. From Astrakhan Russian merchants, sometimes bearing commissions from the Tsar, dispersed throughout the east selling metalwares, weaponry, textiles, and leather goods or bartering sables and other valuable furs.[3] Cossacks and their associates at times shared in these occupations. This thriving commercialism, coupled with the hunting, trapping, and fishing that the cossacks practiced along the rivers of the steppe, afforded the population of the southern borderlands of Russia a viable alternative to the sedentary and constrained agricultural labor of those who remained under Muscovite authority. The mobility that was provided by the expanses of the steppe was matched by the economic differentiation that these various occupations offered. The cossack communities of the southern borderlands became something of a replica, on much smaller scale, of the frontier society that had been Kievan Rus.

It was the natural democracy of the cossack that most determined the special character of the new settlements that sprang up south and southeast of the Muscovite fortified borders. Conscious of the restrictions and deprivations that they had fled, the cossacks created for themselves a military society in which all feelings of exclusiveness based upon racial or

[2]Günter Stökl, *Die Entstehung des Kosakentums* (Munich, 1953), pp. 106–11.
[3]Fuhrmann, pp. 33–34.

ethnic considerations, class origins, or crimes against civilized legal codes, including murder, were rigorously excluded. The renegade who sought sanctuary in cossack lands was never spurned because of his antecedents or habits. Religion alone was the sole possible impediment to acceptance into the cossack ranks, for the Orthodox Church was the common denominator that all had to share. But this condition was easily met. The newcomer was often put to a single test by the ataman of the community. He was asked to demonstrate how he made the sign of the cross, then was requested to state his belief in the divinity of Christ, the Trinity, and other articles of Christian dogma. Passing this investigation immediately admitted the parvenu to full membership in the cossack settlement.[4] As early as the sixteenth century the cossacks of the Don were accepting as comrades Christianized Tatars who wished to exchange service to the khan for a more unbridled way of life along the steppe. Once having accustomed themselves to the cossacks' total disregard for former allegiances and loyalties, these renegades apparently were not at all loath to attack and pillage the villages of their former countrymen.[5]

It is possible, as a recent study has suggested, that many of the cossacks were former galley slaves of the Crimean Tatars and the Turks. Throughout the time of the Mongol yoke thousands of Russians were captured by Tatar raiders for the purpose of selling them into slavery. From the slave marts of the Crimea many of these unfortunates found themselves purchased by Turkish masters, who bound them to service in their war galleys. Some of these slaves apparently were able to flee their Crimean or Turkish captors and make their way to the steppe frontier. During the seventeenth century contemporary sources from among the Don Cossacks report the activities of a certain Katorzhnyi, who was appointed ataman. This surname almost certainly derived from the word *katorga*, a Russian noun of Turkish origin that designated a galley slave. Of all possible sentences that could be imposed upon slaves, service in the galleys was the most feared and hated. If Katorzhnyi was representative of other cossacks who reached the steppe settlements after similar experiences, the passionate love of freedom so evident among the cossacks becomes much more understandable, as does their violent hatred of all forms of law.[6]

Among the cossacks the frontier ethic was the sole law. Every man was

[4]Maurice Hindus, *The Cossacks: The Story of a Warrior People* (Westport, Conn.: Greenwood Press, 1945), pp. 32–33.

[5]Kliuchevsky, *Seventeenth Century,* p. 112.

[6]Lantzeff and Pierce, pp. 75–76. The reader who wishes a brief but stimulating discussion of the origins and spirit of the cossacks will find chapter 5 of this work very useful.

expected to serve the community and to use his special aptitudes for the good of his fellows. Each was expected to be brave and effective in battle. All were to live by their own labor and to provide for the common good. An unwritten but rigidly observed law banned all agricultural work and threatened with the penalty of death anyone who violated this injunction. Cossacks were to support themselves by hunting, fishing, beekeeping, raising animals, and other nomadic pursuits. Tilled lands were prohibited in cossack settlements because farming bound men to a single location. Farm plots could not be concealed from the agents of state authority. Agriculture was an open invitation to bondage.[7] The Don Cossacks continued to ban farming as an occupation until the end of the seventeenth century. The Cossacks of the Yaik had scant acquaintance with agriculture until the eighteenth century and subsisted primarily on a diet of fresh, dried, and salted fish.[8]

Like all frontiersmen, the cossacks valued the strong and effective individual and rewarded him with positions of leadership. But those entrusted with positions of responsibility were expected to exhibit the same distaste for authority over his fellows that every cossack felt. The community was ruled by an ataman (or hetman, as he was known among the Ukrainian cossacks), who was elected by the cossack assembly. Judges and other functionaries were similarly elected by their comrades. The man chosen to be ataman was expected, like Caesar (or Boris Godunov), to decline the appointment at least twice. The most favored candidate was he who had to be dragged, kicking and shouting imprecations, before the assembly. Even then the elders of the cossack host would impress upon him the contempt that his fellows felt for all authority by heaping mud upon his head. An ataman or any other elected official who proved lax in discharging his responsibilities or who developed too strong an appreciation of his own power was dispatched summarily by the assembly. Often the shirt of such an official would be heavily loaded with sand and its wearer cast into the river, where the rushing waters could hide forever his threat to the established cossack norms.[9]

Membership among the cossacks was far from rigid. Those who became dissatisfied with the cossack way of life were free to leave the com-

---

[7] Platonov, *Times of Troubles*, p. 35.

[8] I. G. Rozner, *Yaik pered burei* (Moscow, 1966), pp. 34, 65.

[9] Kliuchevsky, *Seventeenth Century*, p. 115; Philip Longworth, *The Cossacks* (New York: Rinehart and Winston, 1969), p. 37. In recognizing that the southern borderlands acted as a safety valve to which the more explosive elements of Russian society could be vented, Longworth shows that he is one of the few scholars writing on the Russian South with an appreciation of Turner's frontier thesis and its application to early Russian history.

munity. Throughout the sixteenth century and as late as the middle of the seventeenth century, the service registers of the southern borderlands mention many individuals who served in the cossack bands only for brief periods, at times seemingly as part of the process of growing to maturity. Youths who wished to have a fling with the wild and free life of the steppe frequently "went cossacking" with companions before settling down to responsibilities on their estates or in the regular Muscovite army. In 1622 the service register of the town of Elets refers to a group of landowners who, seemingly bored with their lives, temporarily departed their estates for a brief stint of service among the cossacks. When the novelty of such an enterprise vanished (or the rigors of cossack life proved too formidable), they returned to their places of origin, where some became indentured to noblemen and others became lay brothers in local monasteries.[10] As long as such curious newcomers could be of some benefit to the community, the cossacks seem not to have minded these passing visits. The mobility of such adventurers probably enhanced the restlessness and lack of permanence of cossack life and was appreciated for that very reason.

Along the Dnieper-Bug river system, in the settlement known as the Zaporozhie, the ethnic mix in the cossack camps was even more varied. By the latter part of the sixteenth century the population of the Zaporozhie was about four-fifths White Russian and Little Russian origin. The remainder was composed of refugees from the Muscovite state, Poles, Circassians, and Moldavians. Occasionally Tatars, Germans, and Serbs also made their way to the Zaporozhie, although these were rarer.[11] Here all distinctions and allegiances quickly became blurred, and even the religious solidarity insisted upon in other cossack hosts was ignored. The Zaporozhian Cossacks were the first to indicate the prominent historical role that the other cossack bands would play in the future. In 1591 a bankrupt Polish landowner, Christopher Kosinski, who had joined the Zaporozhian forces, consolidated the various resentments that his fellow cossacks felt toward the government of Poland (particularly its default in paying service salaries to cossacks who had been employed as Polish mercenaries) and mounted attacks on Ukrainian border settlements. Kosinski's prime objective was the large estates of local Polish landowners. He presaged the social message of later rebels from the steppe by declaring his intention to be that of slaughtering all noblemen and securing their riches for his comrades in arms. But like his successors, Kosinski found that his fierce but undisciplined forces were no

[10]Kliuchevsky, *Seventeenth Century*, p. 111.
[11]M. Hrushevsky, *Istoriia Ukrainy-Rusi* (Kiev, 1898–1937) 7:155–57.

match for regular military units. Kosinski was killed in combat with the governor of the town of Cherkassy, and his followers were largely massacred or pressed into slavery by their conquerors.[12]

Kosinski's defeat did not deter others from imitating his actions. Fed by runaway peasants from Muscovy and Poland, ruined and disgraced servitors and landholders who were victims of the Oprichnina, common fugitives from justice, adventure-seeking youths from more stable backgrounds and escaped Turkish galley slaves and the foreign prisoners of war who had been settled by the Muscovite government along its borderlands, the steppe had become a tinderbox of explosive material by the early seventeenth century. The stream of refugees southward was swelled by the events of the reign of Boris Godunov. An account from Godunov's time reckons at more than twenty thousand the number of young men of military service age who departed the central provinces of the state to resettle in the Orel-Kromy region. Many undoubtedly continued their flight onto the steppe. Some of these fugitives were made desperate by the crop failures that brought Russia massive famine between 1601 and 1604 and caused starving men to forage for food like packs of wild animals. Some were escaped serfs who used the turmoil caused by the famine to flee their masters. Others were outlaws and bandits whose roving bands had been defeated in battle by regular Muscovite forces. Some were bondmen who had been voluntarily released by their lords because of their inability to feed additional mouths during such hard times. Some were the menials of boyars who had been placed under interdict by Godunov for real or imagined treason and conspiracy against his administration. These domestics were forbidden by Godunov's decree to be assumed by other households and were condemned to perpetual wandering in search of food and shelter. All these replenished the already restive atmosphere of the southern borderlands. None felt any affection or loyalty to the political and social system that had reduced them to ruin.[13]

As long as the Rurikid dynasty had remained in power, disgruntled elements of Muscovite society had accepted the notion that the Tsar was a legal authority, however stern and distasteful that authority might have been, and therefore had not rebelled against his rule. Popular protests had been limited to escape to the frontiers, by "going to the cossacks." But with the ending of the dynasty and the accession of Boris Godunov, the popular attitude toward political power was altered. As Vasily Kliuchevsky has said, the common folk of Russia were at first confused by the disappearance of the dynasty that had ruled them for centuries,

[12]Kliuchevsky, *Seventeenth Century*, p. 119.
[13]Platonov, *Time of Troubles*, pp. 74–75.

then began to realize that they, like the ambitious princes, scheming boyars, and other members of the privileged classes, had a right to stake their claim to participation in any form of rule that replaced the Rurikids.[14] The appearance of the Pseudo-Dmitry presented to the various malcontents of the southern steppe not only their first point of entry into national politics but a banner around which all of them—bondmen and landowners, criminals and former slaves—could rally in their first show of solidarity and mutual support. The restorationist movement of the Pseudo-Dmitry ironically gave the frontier lands their first voice in Russian politics. It is hardly surprising that the Pretender received his greatest support from the town of Putivl, where many of the refugees from Muscovy had congregated to savor their new liberty before embarking upon the still freer but more perilous steppe. That the town of Putivl also later served as the major base of operations for the armies of Ivan Bolotnikov is hardly surprising.[15]

The Pretender's call to arms against Moscow, however, was not answered only by those who had deserted the Muscovite state. The military servitors of the garrison towns along the southern frontier (some of which, such as Livny, Voronezh and Elets, had been founded on orders of Godunov himself) were among the first to respond to the summons of the Pseudo-Dmitry and to march north in his cause. Clearly the frontier spirit and the rebelliousness of the southern inhabitants had made their mark even upon those who had been dispatched to contain their energies.

When the initial success of the Pretender was terminated by his assassination in Moscow, the people of the southern borderlands could not believe that so useful a weapon as pretendership, which had welded their disparate grievances into a concerted political movement, was ineffective and should be abandoned. Even before rumors of a second pretender spread throughout the Russian state, the people of the frontier towns of Riazan, Putivl, and Tula, supported and encouraged by the cossack communities of the steppe, rose in rebellion against Moscow, supposedly in the name of the Pseudo-Dmitry. A fabricated story was mouthed about that Dmitry had once again escaped his would-be murderers and was hiding somewhere in Russia, readying himself for a return to power. But this fiction was probably as incredible to the inhabitants of the south as it is today to undergraduate students. The Polish aristocrats and their Jesuit advisers did not invent the second pretender. They had this phantom thrust upon them from the Russian south. The

[14]Kliuchevsky, *Seventeenth Century*, p. 54.
[15]Paul Avrich, *Russian Rebels, 1600–1800* (New York: Shocken Books, 1972), p. 16.

Thief of Tushino was demanded by the popular will of the southern borderlands.[16]

The Pseudo-Dmitry and his obviously bogus successor were but pale shadows of the frontier personality that soon would crystallize the massive resentment of the frontier lands into a cohesive force strong enough to attempt the complete destruction of the Muscovite political and social system. Such a figure had been active in the Russian south during the first stages of the Time of Troubles but, overshadowed by the formidable personalities that dominated the dynastic phase of this crisis, went largely unnoticed. But the accession of Tsar Vasily Shuisky, who promised to ensure the predominance of the boyar class and their privileged status, brought this new leader to the fore. This man, who became the figurehead of all later enemies of the Muscovite social system, was the cossack ataman Ivan Bolotnikov.

Bolotnikov came to the steppe in possession of many of the skills and much of the charisma of the Roman slave leader Spartacus. During his early youth Bolotnikov had been the slave of Prince Andrei Teliatevsky, a boyar military officer who, struck by Bolotnikov's natural gifts, had introduced him to military pursuits as part of his normal duties. But Bolotnikov was unable to abide even a favorable form of bondage. He escaped from Teliatevsky's service and joined cossack bands on the steppe, where the freedom and violence of frontier life were greatly to his liking. Bolotnikov was another of the inhabitants of the south who served an apprenticeship in Turkish galleys. Captured by raiding Tatar horsemen, he was sold into slavery to the Turks and, because of his remarkable strength, was assigned to slavery in the Turkish navy as an oarsman. His intelligence elevated him above the sad lot of his fellow slaves and secured for him the comparatively lofty position of helmsman of a Turkish warship. During a naval engagement Bolotnikov's ship was captured intact by German sailors, who, following the custom of Westerners who fought the Turks, freed the galley slaves of the Turkish vessel. Bolotnikov then attempted to return to the steppe by way of Poland. But while in Poland he learned of the designs of the supporters of the Pseudo-Dmitry and joined their forces. Known as a brave and strong warrior capable of mastering the skills of command and strategy, Bolotnikov was sent by the Pretender's Polish accomplices to southern Russia, where he was enjoined to foment rebellion and arouse popular support for Dmitry's cause. Bolotnikov arrived in Putivl after Dmitry's death. But he continued to

---

[16]Kliuchevsky, *History*, 3:37.

pose as a supporter of the Pretender and helped fan the rumor that Dmitry was still alive and preparing for a return to power.[17]

In and around the town of Putivl were perhaps as many as twenty thousand runaway bondmen and fugitive serfs. Some of these, like Bolotnikov himself, had gained some military experience by serving former masters in various capacities of a military nature.[18] With these and the help of local military servitors, Bolotnikov was able to mount an oppositionist movement of sufficient might and credibility that it attracted the support of uprooted and dispossessed princely and boyar families who had been the chief victims of Ivan the Terrible's Oprichnina. Many of these had been exiled to the southern sectors of the Russian state and had their own scores to settle with the Muscovite ruling circles.[19] But these more aristocratic segments of Bolotnikov's movement could not have expressed their opposition openly, had not the peoples of the steppe provided the massive support that gave this rebellion its hope of success.

Amid the terror and barbarism that Bolotnikov's uprising unleashed upon Russia, a more purposeful note was sounded and was not lost upon the Muscovite government: the opponents of the regime could now be coordinated in their opposition and were not averse to realizing their suppressed desires by destroying the very foundations of Muscovite political power. All future Russian rulers had to calculate the influence of the frontier in any national undertaking. Russia was thereafter haunted not so much by the "specter of social revolution" that writers seldom fail to mention, but rather the spirit of the frontier. Inarticulate, often self-contradictory, the aspirations of the frontiersmen never coalesced into a counterideology powerful enough to supplant the political and social creeds upon which Moscow based its power. But the values treasured by the frontiersman were real enough and, on proper occasion, sufficiently inflammatory to plunge Russia into terrible civil war.

Bolotnikov's forces were defeated and he himself paid for his rashness with his life. But Moscow was forced by his jacquerie to adopt stringent safeguards against similar movements. During the reigns of Michael and Alexis Romanov the government once again increased the fortifications of the steppe frontier by relocating the basic lines of defensive garrisons several hundred miles farther south. But because of the disruptions caused by the Time of Troubles, the state could not prevent new peasant migrations to the lands immediately to the rear of this line. Attempts to

[17] Avrich, pp. 20–21. V. N. Aleksandrenko, "Materialy po smutnomu vremeni na Rusi XVII v.," *Starina i novizna* 14 (1911):262–63.

[18] I. I. Smirnov, *Vosstanie Bolotnikova, 1606–1607* 2nd ed. (Moscow, 1951), pp. 107–9.

[19] Avrich, pp. 32–33.

defeat surviving bands of brigands throughout central Russia, war with Poland, and other distractions prevented more forceful administration of affairs in the countryside. Hundreds of peasants fled southward, traveling openly along their route, taking with them their relatives, livestock, and belongings, while their lords were absent from their estates fulfilling demands of their obligation to military service. Many of these refugees were rather prosperous, not at all the poorest elements of the peasantry. Their exodus cost the Muscovite treasury, already strained by many demands, to lose important sources of needed revenue.[20] The drain of manpower from service estates prompted service landholders to petition Moscow that further programs for the fortification and pacification of the southern borderlands be de-emphasized.[21] But total compliance with this request would deny the government any opportunity to practice a dynamic foreign policy toward the khan of the Crimea. Instead, the government of Tsar Alexis began to rely upon legal and administrative enactments to terminate peasant flight to the south. The first fruit of this new course of action was the famous *Ulozhenie* of 1649, which ratified as law of the land the total immobility of the population.

Today it is customary to argue that the significance of the *Ulozhenie* to the growth of serfdom in Russia has been overstressed by earlier generations of historians. Serfdom, the argument goes, existed throughout Russia long before Tsar Alexis made it a formal law through this legislation. Thus the code of 1649 merely stated publicly what had long been an accomplished fact: the serf was bound to his occupation and was locked to his plot of land as the chattel of his master. But the evidence of the sizeable migrations that preceded the *Ulozhenie* testify to the inability of the Muscovite government to restrain the mobility of the working forces. Each time the southern fortifications were advanced into the steppe, masses of peasants were not wanting to fill the new lands that were thereby made safe for settlement. Serfdom had indeed existed before Tsar Alexis's day; the problem was rather that of making the Russian people accept their enserfed condition and remain in their place.

The *Ulozhenie* was a response to a definite and serious threat to Moscow's continued viability, the call of the frontier to those wishing new opportunities in a new land, and the deleterious influence that the frontier

---

[20] I. A. Bulygin, "Beglye krest'iane Riazanskogo uezda v 60-e gody XVII v.," *Istoricheskie zapiski* 42 (1953): 131–49; N. A. Baklanova, "Dela o syske beglykh krest'ian i kholopov kak istochnik dlia istorii tiaglogo sel'skogo naseleniia v Povolzhe vo vtoroi polovine XVII v.," *Problemy istochnikovedeniia* 11 (1963): 314–16. See also Hellie, pp. 127–28.

[21] A. A. Novosel'sky, *Bor'ba moskovskogo gosudarstva s tatarami v pervoi polovine XVII veka* (Moscow-Leningrad, 1948), pp. 300–305.

promised to exert upon subsequent Russian history. Moscow could no longer allow itself the convenience of permitting potential rebels to resettle on the frontier, for now the frontier had demonstrated that it could mold such rebels into a concentrated force highly dangerous to the state. The later rebellion of Stenka Razin underscored this circumstance. But the opening of Siberia made the full development of the service state even more imperative, even as it raised anew problems that the Muscovite government had hoped were resolved.

VII. The Siberian Safety Valve

THE ENSERFMENT OF the Russian peasant ironically coincided with the opening of a vast new frontier for the Russian state, an expanse of free land so immense that it seemed to offer free farming land without limit, personal enterprise without end, and boundless opportunities for personal advancement and mobility. In addition, the new colony of Siberia was a veritable treasure trove. Even Ivan the Terrible, who at first was vexed by the drive of Ermak's cossacks beyond the Urals (probably because he understood at once that those who dreaded his Oprichnina and his other abuses of power would quit their homesites and seek in the east a new way of life), was quick to realize the economic significance of Siberia. The rich new sources of furs reported by the cossacks were of paramount importance to the Russian state budget, for these furs were of such high quality that they commanded high prices not only at home but on foreign markets as well.[1] Within a century of Ermak's initial thrusts into Siberia, Moscow was realizing a profit from the Siberian fur trade of approximately three hundred and fifty thousand rubles annually. In terms of the Russian economy of 1913, the figure was equal to about five or six million gold rubles.[2] Here was reason enough for the Russian government to run any risk, including that of disrupting its newly enserfed populace, to seize this unexpected source of gain.

There was yet another reason for Russian interest in Siberia, one that has been noted in other connections. The constant pressure that the frontier had exerted upon the Russian state undoubtedly motivated Russian officials to grasp this opportunity to expand its lines of defense so far from the Muscovite heartlands that disasters originating from beyond their borders would forever be precluded. The attacks of frontier enemies had always necessitated retaliatory and defensive raids along the Russian borders; it was but a short step to turn these reflexive operations into full-

---

[1] *Istoriia Sibiri* (Leningrad, 1968), 2: 9–22.

[2] R. H. Fisher, *The Russian Fur Trade, 1550–1700* (Berkeley, Calif.: University of California Press, 1943), p. 181; George Vernadsky, *The Tsardom of Moscow, 1547–1682* (New Haven: Yale University Press, 1969), 1: 307.

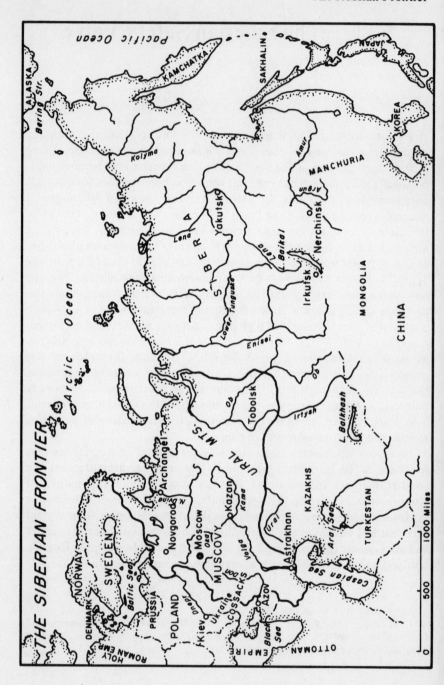

scale offensive campaigns of an imperialistic nature.[3] By the reign of Boris Godunov the decision to conquer as much of Siberia as possible had been reached. Using Ermak's holdings in western Siberia as a base of operations and supply, the Russians launched an unprecedented overland advance that secured for Moscow an expanse of territory much greater than that which later drew American homesteaders westward to the Pacific.

Siberia offered its colonists a landscape of unbelievable proportions, a totally new horizon to replace what had been obscured for centuries by the limited perspectives of life in the forest zone. Settlers beyond the Urals were forced to undertake an entirely new beginning, for in embarking upon the vast reaches of Siberia, they severed all connection with the lands of their birth. Here they found no ties to the past, a land without history, a clean slate upon which entirely new forms could be inscribed. Memories of earlier times and ancient customs and habits were replaced by hopes and dreams of the future, a future that promised to be as limitless as the Siberian wilderness itself.

It is significant that the Muscovite state owed the conquest of Siberia not to its own designs and the application of its military strength but to private initiative and free enterprise. The commercial family of the Stroganovs first conceived the plan of conquest and financed Ermak and his cossacks for its implementation. After Ermak's troops had broken the resistance of local Siberian natives, individuals and groups of traders and trappers followed in their wake, seeking new sources of furs and new tribes of natives upon whom tribute could be imposed. Only then came the military servitors and those who collected for the Muscovite state its tribute in fur, known as the *yasak,* which became obligatory for all Siberians who fell under Moscow's domination. Finally came more sedate colonists, who wished to exploit the arable land of the region, and the officials of the church. This process continued in successive new surges across Siberia until the Pacific was reached. Free enterprise and daring individuals blazed the trails eastward, incorporating one river system after another into the Russian state. Representatives of official Russia were content to leave the many risks to private citizens and satisfied themselves with the rewards that could be gathered in more orderly and less adventurous fashion in their rear. Those in the vanguard of this colonizing movement enjoyed opportunity for living the life of the frontiersman that Russia had not seen since the fall of Kiev.

[3]Alton S. Donnelly, *The Russian Conquest of Bashkiria, 1552-1740* (New Haven: Yale University Press, 1968), p. 3; Kerner, p. 68.

Moscow hoped that the influx of colonists needed for the settlement of the new colony could be rigidly controlled. During the sixteenth century, therefore, the Muscovite government directed the entire process of relocation, forcibly resettling or exiling whole families of peasants to Siberia when their labor was needed. But many of these unwilling settlers died on the way. Many managed to escape their supervisors and take up permanent residence in one or another of the garrison towns through which they passed on route. Some even escaped state service completely and either made their way farther eastward, where the government had not yet established outposts and garrisons, or returned to their homes in European Russia.[4] Local Siberian military governors, always troubled by a lack of soldiers to man their garrisons, also recruited peasants in Great Russia to settle their posts or work neighboring farmland. These officials were also known to conceal from higher Muscovite authorities runaways who appeared in their jurisdictions and who were willing to serve in their garrisons.[5]

Before and after the Time of Troubles the Russian government also continued its practice of resettling foreign prisoners of war along frontiers to derive benefit from their military expertise. Swedes, Poles, Livonians, Lithuanians, and other captives were deported east of the Urals, where some willingly accepted permanent service in the Russian army and pursued lifelong careers in Siberia. Native criminals were also relocated to Siberia at this time. By 1645 as many as fifteen hundred could be found among the Russian settlers.[6] It is indicative of the concerns of the government that peasants recruited for resettlement to Siberia were not chosen from areas where serfdom had long been entrenched. Most often such peasants were gathered from the Russian north and from outlying regions already acquainted with the conditions of frontier life, such as from the town of Perm.[7]

Soviet scholars have often argued that agriculture in Siberia from the start was made to conform to the principles of Great Russia and that native Russians who found themselves in Siberia during the first generations of its development were serfs, convicts, and others, who were sent "in shackles." But the truth of the matter seems quite different.[8] Before 1645

[4] *Istoriia Sibiri*, 2: 64.
[5] Ibid., p. 38.
[6] Vernadsky, *Tsardom of Moscow*, 1: 183; P. N. Butsinsky, *Zaselenie Sibiri i byt eia pervykh nasel'nikov* (Kharkov, 1889), p. 199.
[7] Butsinky, *Zaselenie Sibiri*, p. 231.
[8] See the comments of Donald W. Treadgold, "Russian Expansion in the Light of Turner's Study of the American Frontier," *Agricultural History* 26 (Oct. 1952): 149.

the Muscovite government relocated to Siberia about eight thousand peasant families.[9] By that date, however, the total number of Russian males throughout Siberia was about seventy thousand.[10] When one subtracts from this figure the number of official military and administrative servitors in the Siberian service (a number that was, as we shall see, surprisingly small), one can conclude that perhaps one-third of all Russians in Siberia arrived there by unofficial means. These were the so-called wandering people *(guliashchie liudi),* who in one way or another had escaped their landlords and crossed the Urals of their own accord. Inasmuch as many of these illegal immigrants fled to totally unsupervised parts or hid themselves from all Muscovite functionaries, the number of such refugees in Siberia may have been quite high. Clearly, Siberia functioned as a safety valve during the first half-century of its colonization and rivaled the steppe borderlands in attracting dissident and disgusted segments of Russian society. Probably Siberia also came under consideration when the government of Tsar Alexis decided to restrict peasant movement by enactment of the *Ulozhenie.*

During and after the schism in the Russian church, Old Believers swelled the population of Siberia by thousands. Judging from local reports of the activities of schismatics in Siberia, their numbers in some settlements were large. Local sources speak of a congregation of several thousand Old Believers in the region of the river Ob. When government suppression of their community and attempts to convert them to Orthodoxy followed them to their new abodes, some twenty-seven hundred schismatics reportedly burned themselves alive during a single year (1679) rather than alter their views and betray their convictions.[11] If these dissidents were able to flee to Siberia in such large numbers, we can believe that large numbers of simpler folk were also able to strike out for the east even after the promulgation of the *Ulozhenie.*

Muscovite officials in Siberia during the early seventeenth century were severely perplexed by the relatively few peasants under their jurisdiction. These colonial administrators attempted to convince or coerce the native populace to forsake their traditional nomadic pursuits in favor of agricultural work that would supply the food supplies badly needed by Russian garrisons.[12] But the Siberian, loath to embark upon a path that

[9]George Vernadsky, "O dvizhenii russkikh na vostok," *Nauchnyi istoricheskii zhurnal* 12 (1914): 59.

[10]P. A. Slovtsov, *Istoricheskoe obozrenie Sibiri,* 2d ed. (Saint Petersburg, 1886), 1:84–85.

[11]G. V. Glinka, ed., *Aziatskaia Rossiia, I: Liudi i poriadki za Uralom* (Saint Petersburg, 1914), p. 204.

[12]G. F. Miller, *Istoriia Sibiri* (Moscow, 1937), p. 383.

could lead only to increased governmental interference in their lives, if not to eventual enserfment, refused to provide for the subsistence of the servitors who followed the progression of the Russian frontier eastward. In 1601 the Muscovite government could claim but twelve agricultural settlements at their disposal in all their Siberian holdings.[13] Throughout the century this situation improved little. Siberian governors were forced to import grain and other foodstuffs from European Russia and to transport these goods to places as far distant as the Pacific coast. This system of supply often required as many as five years to reach its goal, by which time spoilage had cost a great percentage of the original shipment.[14]

Once again Moscow found it necessary to loosen its control of its peasantry to achieve expansionist aims. Lest complete prohibition of resettlement deny Siberian administrative units the colonists needed and thereby imperil the rich fur trade, limited numbers of peasants were allowed to relocate in western Siberia. Government records of the early years of the eighteenth century show that in western Siberia peasants and artisans far surpassed the number of state servitors. In 1701 western Siberia had 6,442 families that belonged to the class of servitors and 1,994 families that were townsfolk. For the same date, however, 9,342 peasant families are recorded.[15] Official information for 1710 reports that in the district of Tobolsk 29,423 peasants were among the 41,437 males living in the settlements (*slobody*) of the district.[16] Although these new residents probably had also been selected from the old frontier regions of the Muscovite state, their presence in Siberia created communities of frontier farmers from whom a new frontier spirit and new frontier institutions might have arisen.

But the Russian government was careful to ensure that western Siberia did not become a land of free enterprise and democracy that would beckon to enserfed peasants throughout the Russian Empire. The marriage of agriculture and service in western Siberia was soon consummated. Muscovite servitors were compensated by the state not with salaries or supplies of grain but through grants of land, estates on which the newly migrating peasants and peasants sent by the government were made to settle. The notion that use of land depended upon service to the

---

[13]*Istoriia Sibiri*, 2:37.

[14]V. I. Shunkov, *Ocherki po istorii zemledeliia Sibiri (XVII v.)* (Moscow, 1956), p. 314.

[15]*Istoriia Sibiri*, 2: 39.

[16]V. I. Shunkov, *Ocherki po istorii kolonizatsii Sibiri v XVII-nachale XVIII v.* (Moscow-Leningrad, 1946), p. 116.

state thus followed the Russian peasant to his new homesite.[17] Simultaneously, the natives of western Siberia were coerced into a new way of life. Hitherto they had favored paying their taxes to the Russian state in the form of furs, for such an arrangement left them free to continue their nomadic occupations. But now a tax in kind, in grain, was demanded, forcing the western Siberian to undertake agricultural work. Like his counterparts in Great Russia, the western Siberian became a state peasant.[18] Through these measures western Siberia in time was brought under the control of Muscovite institutions so thoroughly that the frontier spirit of its original populace withered, and the danger that aspirations toward a freer form of life would be transmitted through this medium to the Russian interior was dispelled.

Control of this kind was not possible throughout the extensive area of subsequent Russian colonization. Frederick Jackson Turner once said of the American frontier experience that as the western frontier continued to advance, frontiersmen who followed it continually left behind them more settled societies and continually returned to primitive conditions. On an expanding frontier, Turner noted, social development tends to repeat itself in ever-new surroundings. Yesterday's attempts to enforce rigid centralization are undermined by today's new experiences in freshly settled wastelands. This was true also of Siberia. As the Russian frontier continued to push eastward, the Muscovite regime was unable to thwart free enterprise and the full play of dynamic individualism in outlying regions. In the van of the colonizing movement, customs of life and forms of activity inimicable to staid Muscovite practice were constantly being reborn. At the same time, new safety valves were appearing in succession for those who had recently been subjected to control in lands that had been settled much earlier. The more restive and bolder peasants of western Siberia, joined by new runaways from central Russia and dispirited members of the native populace, were able to flee eastward to lands still totally free from centralized order and the idea of service obligations.

In the eastern outreaches of the Siberian continent, independence and self-reliance were enhanced by a remoteness from the seats of Russian state power that caused the extension of Muscovite institutions to falter.

[17] Donnelly, p. 29; V. E. Den, *Naselenie Rossii po piatoi revizii: Podushnaia podat' v XVIII veke i statistika naseleniia v kontse XVIII veka* (Moscow, 1902), 2, pt. 2: 178.

[18] Ronald F. Drew, "The Emergence of an Agricultural Policy for Siberia in the XVII and XVIII Centuries," *Agricultural History* 33 (Jan. 1959): 29–32; Butsinsky, *Zaselenie Sibiri,* pp. 168–69.

This remoteness also bred sentiments of rebellion that helped to ensure that Siberia would escape total subordination to Moscow's wishes. During the seventeenth century Siberia witnessed scores of major upheavals and uprisings against local authorities and their attempts to subject settlers and native inhabitants to the needs of the state. Although these insurrections invariably were defeated, they did impress upon the Russian government the need to tread lightly throughout the east and to forgo efforts to impose anything resembling full serfdom upon the laboring classes of Siberia.[19]

For this reason serfdom was almost wholly unknown in Siberia until after 1750. By the end of the seventeenth century only about 14 percent of the peasantry of Siberia (west and east alike) had lost the right to leave their lands. These were, for the most part, peasants who had attached themselves to monastery lands and, in return for a sheltered existence, had forsworn their right to resettle elsewhere. The remainder of the peasant population was recorded in government dossiers as "black people," or later as "state peasants." Such people were secure in their personal freedom but had to discharge some labor obligation imposed by the local governor in the name of the Russian state. Even for these the imposed obligations were slighter than what was expected of state peasants to the west of the Urals. During the seventeenth century the amount of obligatory agricultural work demanded by lords or performed for the state (the so-called *barshchina* labor) actually decreased throughout Siberia.[20]

The Muscovite administration of Siberia remained quite different from what it was in European Russia. Inasmuch as Siberia had become part of the Russian Empire rather late in its history, many of the traditional semifeudal practices of early Russian political life had already been discredited and were not transferred to Siberia. Noticeably absent was the widely despised system of *kormlenie,* the allowance to local officials of the right to secure the means of their own upkeep and livelihood through taxes, customs, and other fiscal impositions on citizens under their juris-

---

[19]On these uprisings, see Z. Ya. Boiarshinova, "Volneniia v Tomske v XVII veke," *Voprosy istorii,* 1956, no. 2, pp. 112 ff.; O. V. Ionova, *Iz istorii Yakutskogo naroda (pervaia polovina XVII veka)* (Yakutsk, 1945), pp. 79–91; F. A. Kudriavtsev, *Vosstaniia krest'ian, posadskikh i kazakov v vostochnoi Sibiri v kontse XVII v.* (Irkutsk, 1939), pp. 38–85. The great social upheaval led by Stenka Razin also was reflected in Siberia through local discontent and rioting; see George Lantzeff, *Siberia in the Seventeenth Century* (New York: Octagon Books, 1972), p. 83.

[20]D. M. Golovachev, "Chastnoe zemlevladenie v Sibiri," *Sibirskie voprosy,* 1905, no. 1, p. 125; B. Nolde, *La formation de l'empire Russe* (Paris, 1952–53), 1: 174–84; *Istoriia Sibiri,* 2: 152.

diction. This practice, which Ivan the Terrible had abolished as part of his early domestic reforms, was not applied to Siberian administration. Moscow also saw that too much power was not concentrated in any single Siberian official. Although this step was undoubtedly taken to prevent the rise of strongmen who could challenge Muscovite authority and attempt secession from the empire, it was not without benefit to Siberian residents, who chafed under any form of authority. Moscow also attempted to prevent extortions and exploitation of the people of Siberia by strictly limiting the "voluntary gifts" that Russian officials could acquire while holding office.[21] From the start the Russian government made it known that Siberia was not to become a land of personal fiefs for ambitious lords wishing to carve out their own empires and bureaucrats desiring unchecked power over their charges. Although many of these injunctions were readily violated, as we shall soon see, the administrative life of Siberia did attempt to avoid needless provocation of the citizenry through injustices and imperviousness to local desires and values.

[21]Lantzeff, pp. 24–25.

VIII. The Frontier Life of Siberia

THE REALITIES of Siberian life were totally antithetical to the established norms of Russian national life. There was no way in which the Russian government could have forced its will upon this great semicontinent, which was far larger than European Russia. The serfdom, autocracy, and service mentality that had shaped the destiny of Great Russia could not be incorporated into this new colony. On every side there were sanctuaries throughout Siberia in which those who opposed Muscovite ways could hide themselves and follow their own inclinations. In dealing with this great vacuum, the Russian state was forced to adapt itself to new resourcefulness and enterprise. The dream of assimilating this massive giant was early recognized as vanity; a secondary objective, that of preserving Muscovite institutions from influence by this new and troubling neighbor, was more feasible and received more direct attention by Moscow. Consequently, Moscow adopted a policy of allowing limited laissez-faire and permitting limited autonomy throughout eastern Siberia, while striving to ensure that western Siberia remained under Muscovite control and therefore unlikely to become a conductor of eastern frontier influences to the Russian heartland. It is this factor, and not the doings of governments or individuals, that has made Siberian life different from the rest of the Russian Empire even to this day. And for this reason the inhabitants of Siberia have enjoyed self-determination of their local affairs and self-sufficiency that has long been lost to their western neighbors.

As was later to be the case in the American West, the colonization of Siberia was the work of civilians. Military forces were only auxiliary to this process. The initial work of exploration, the first interaction with natives, the initiation of the first fur trade, and the institution of the notion that tribute should be paid to Russian overlords were all accomplished by intrepid frontiersmen, most of whom lacked any official commission for their work. These enterprisers were followed by army units that assumed control over the newly settled region and began to regulate its economic life, subordinating private objectives to the purposes of the state whenever possible and maintaining a military presence that urged the natives to fulfill the obligations imposed upon them. Thus, Russian military forces entered areas that already bore the stamp of free enterprise. The

Russian military servitors followed in the tracks of men so intrepid that they could not fail to be impressed by their qualities and their achievements. It is hardly surprising that they quickly came to emulate their spirit of resourcefulness and to wish for themselves something of their unrestrained way of life.

The advance into eastern Siberia was led by Russian traders and hunters who were called *promyshlenniki*. Often compared to the Canadian *Coureurs de Bois* because of their intrepidity and ruthless methods, these private enterprisers either pursued their own objectives in the wilds or were employed by other commercialists for the purpose of discovering and exploiting new sources of fur. When business was slow, they were occasionally chartered by local governors of Russian towns to go among wild tribesmen to collect the official *yasak*. But the *promyshlenniki* preferred to operate in their own private capacities and for their own gain. Organized in small armed bands known as *vatagas*, they plunged into uncharted territory well in advance of the Russian military advance, hoping to gain the best furs to be found in new lands. Each *vataga* was a sort of joint-stock company, in which every member of the band was guaranteed an equal share of the booty that resulted from their common efforts. Needing their experience and impressed by their daring, the Russian government allowed them full latitude to go where they wished and to amass private fortunes. Their sole command from Moscow was simple: "To collect the *yasak* and to seek new lands." Within the limits of this injunction lay opportunity aplenty for personal enrichment, high adventure, and a way of life that knew no limitations, even those of the common codes of morality.[1] These operations beyond the confines of civilization frequently attracted the services of men who in more settled surroundings would have been regarded the most depraved criminal element in society.

Once the *promyshlenniki* had entered a new region, scouted its lands and rivers, and determined its wealth, they were followed by independent bands of military servitors, usually cossacks. Since Ermak's day Moscow had continued to rely upon cossacks for duty in Siberia, recruiting for this purpose members of the cossack settlements along the Don River and other sectors of the steppe. The regular military servitors who accompanied them eastward were most often drawn from the Russian north, the Pomorie region, where the government had also recruited the peasants

[1]George Vernadsky, "Gosudarevy sluzhilye i promyshlennye liudi v vostochnoi Sibiri XVII veka," *Zhurnal ministerstva narodnago prosveshcheniia*, n. s. 61 (1915): 342; Vernadsky, *Tsardom of Moscow*, 1:297; Fisher, pp. 32–33.

who had been resettled in western Siberia. Here again Moscow relied upon its practice of using those already versed in frontier life for duty beyond the Urals and avoided exposing to the frontier servitors of the enserfed and well-regulated central Russian provinces. These soldiers were forced to make the trek into Siberia with their families and with little or no financial assistance from the Russian treasury.[2] Constrained to live off the land as they progressed, the cossacks and their companions did not hesitate to begin the freebooting that life in Siberia promised. Inhabitants of towns that lay in the path of these detachments reacted as to a hostile invader. Town dwellers often hid themselves (or at least their female relatives), secluded their cattle in the woods, and secured their homes as though for a military siege. In many places townspeople prepared provisions for the marchers well in advance of their arrival, in the hope that quick satisfaction of their immediate needs would prompt them to continue their journey without pause. Even with these precautions, however, abuses of the local populace, including pillage, rape, and murder, were common.[3]

Once settled in their garrisons, the military units of Siberia were commissioned to preserve order and to guard against hostile incursions. They were also responsible for seeing that the *yasak* was dutifully received by the Russian government. In return for this service they received compensation in salary and arable land. But these were the least significant inducements for service in Siberia. During their free time the cossacks were allowed to acquire additional land or to traffic in furs, apparently free from all supervision. In reality, most cossacks could be distinguished from the *promyshlenniki* who had preceded them only with difficulty. Also operating in *vatagas,* the cossacks fed upon what remained in the rear of the pioneers and rivaled the latter in the abuses they perpetrated upon native Siberians to obtain their share of the valuable furs.[4]

Like the *promyshlenniki,* the cossacks found it possible to extract riches from the wilderness and its people almost at will. Cossack detachments sent to Siberia usually were so small in number that each individual was important to his garrison; the derelictions of each had to be overlooked, because of the need to keep each fighting man in his place. The conquest of Siberia, like the conquest of Mexico, was accomplished by very small groups of men who functioned often without the assistance and

[2]Lantzeff, pp. 72–73; Butsinsky, *Zaselenie Sibiri,* p. 191.

[3]Lantzeff, pp. 73–74; Butsinsky, *Zaselenie Sibiri,* pp. 191–92; N. N. Ogloblin, *Obozrenie stolbtsov i knig sibirskago prikaza, 1592–1768 gg.* (Moscow, 1895–1900) 3: 2.

[4]Fisher, pp. 29–31; Vernadsky, *Tsardom of Moscow,* 1: 297.

even the knowledge of their government. A petition from the garrison of Yakutsk on the Lena River, written to higher authorities in 1646, illustrates how few servitors prominent garrisons had at their disposal even at that late date in the colonization of Siberia. The commanders of the town requested additional service men and firearms needed to preserve their position. Warning that their forces were badly outnumbered by the local tribesmen from whom they collected tribute, the commanders suggested that they felt insecure even before the threats of their own soldiers. At the time of their petition they listed in the garrison 395 service men and five boyars. These were supported by three ecclesiastics, four specialists in gunmaking and metalworking, and two interpreters. The petitioners reminded their superiors that when detachments from the fort were sent into the hinterland to collect furs from the natives during the winter months, only 50 servitors remained to guard the garrison.[5]

In such surroundings opportunities for dereliction of duty and crass neglect of the basic principles of human decency were plentiful. Contemporary records are suffused with accounts of those who took advantage of their primitive conditions to revert to barbarism. Russian military commanders in Siberia and their administrative counterparts became as renowned for their licentiousness, cupidity, and general moral debasement as had some of the cossack communities of the steppe. Free from the scrutiny of Moscow, officials in eastern Siberia disported themselves in every sort of vice, particularly those that could yield a profit. Their traffic in women was so well known in central Russia that the Russian government eventually came to resent its exclusion from such a lucrative source of revenue and imposed a levy of 10 percent of the gain realized from the selling of women. Siberian officers were not above gambling away or selling their own wives and daughters for profit. Extortion from the natives was commonplace. Often local governors kept for themselves the finest furs that natives surrendered in payment of the *yasak* and sent poorer specimens on to Moscow. Government subsidies were regularly diverted into the pockets of Siberian officials, who then falsified records to conceal their crimes. Furs worth thousands of rubles were illegally exported to European Russia by such criminals, who used relatives, merchants, and other intermediaries to transport this contraband. Nepotism was practiced seemingly on a large scale. Governors brought to Si-

[5]N. S. Orlova, *Otkrytiia russkikh zemleprokhodtsev i poliarnykh morekhodov XVII veka na severo-vostoke Azii* (Moscow, 1951), pp. 212–16.

beria relatives and friends, whom they helped to aggrandize themselves at
the expense of Siberian natives, local Russians, and the treasury of the
Russian state.[6]

Russian soldiers in the garrisons emulated the moral depravity of their
superiors. Gambling and the distilling of liquor were widespread. Servitors robbed and otherwise oppressed the populace they had been appointed to protect. Women from tribal communities and even Russian
women were stolen and sold into slavery. Mutiny was a constant fear of
the Siberian high command. Often drunk or annoyed soldiers would
murder their commanding officers, pillage their towns, then flee to lands
farther east, where the authority of Moscow was still weak and reprisals
could be taken only on rare occasions. In eastern Siberia many renegades
of this sort were so unmotivated by considerations of patriotism or loyalty
that they frequently fled across the Chinese border, then used this
sanctuary as a base from which they conducted raids upon Russian communities, traders, and *promyshlenniki.*[7] Native Siberian tribesmen,
seeing no hope for protection under the law administered by such
miscreants, often resorted to violence in self-defense. Uprisings against
Muscovite officials were common, as was the murder of local officials,
collectors of the *yasak,* and *promyshlenniki.* The despair to which the
rapacious policies of the Russian frontiersmen could reduce the native Siberian is testified to by the mass suicide of many Ostiak tribesmen in
1627, who leaped into the river from their boats during a demonstration
against Muscovite tyranny and drowned themselves in protest, much in
the manner of the Old Believers.[8]

Cossacks who served in the towns of Siberia also exhibited that same
insubordination and disdain for authority that were so prevalant among
their comrades on the steppe. It was not unusual for servitors in Siberia
to refuse to render further service until their salaries were paid or other
abuses rectified. Complaints against commanders were the mildest form
of displeasure cossack frontiersmen could display. Violent reprisals
against unpopular officers, threats, and occasional murder came to be
considered part of the life of the commander assigned to a cossack out-

[6]F. A. Golder, *Russian Expansion on the Pacific, 1641–1850* (New York: Arthur H.
Clark, 1971), pp. 19–21.

[7]Ibid., pp. 19, 22.

[8]Lantzeff, pp. 110–14; Ogloblin, 3: 175. For further examples of the oppression and extortions perpetrated by Russian officials in Siberia, see B. Chicherin, *Oblastnyia uchrezhdeniia
Rossii v XVII veke* (Moscow, 1856), pp. 381–83.

post in Siberia. At times entire garrisons with disputed mutual claims to the local sources of furs waged open warfare against each other. Other garrisons rebelled and, with or without the assistance of their officers, led campaigns of conquest against other Russian outposts.[9] Officials in Moscow and even the Tsar himself were not spared the charges and incriminations of Siberian cossacks. One popular form of protest to Moscow was the threat that unless certain requests were granted, the garrison might desert the Muscovite service completely and form its own republic in some remote corner of Siberia. The cossacks of Siberia also emulated the hosts of the Don and the Zaporozhie by summoning democratic assemblies (known as *krugi* on the steppe and in Siberia as well) to consolidate their grievances and make common representation to commanders. Not infrequently did such assemblies inspire further sedition and incited cossack bands to withdraw from the garrison and establish new cossack communities elsewhere.[10]

When Moscow's reaction to such insubordination proved weak, cossack garrisons began to demand the right to elect their own commanders. In 1632 the town of Tobolsk petitioned the government to honor the right of its servitors to choose their own officers. On this occasion the government withdrew the commander it had assigned to the town and allowed the appointment of a local ataman. There were other instances in which Moscow consulted cossack detachments before naming officers in their outposts. In smaller and more remote garrisons servitors demanded, and apparently received, the right to debate policies announced by the government.[11] By the second half of the seventeenth century the governors of the towns of Siberia were beginning to imitate the independence and disobedience of their charges. In 1671 the military governor (*voevoda*) of Tomsk was summoned to Tobolsk to answer charges preferred against him by his own townspeople. The *voevoda* fulfilled Moscow's command by appearing at Tobolsk; but for two years thereafter he refused to submit to trial by the local *voevoda,* denying the right of another *voevoda* to exercise judgment over him.[12] Although local Siberian politics were primarily responsible for this occurrence, a similar act of insubordination would not have been countenanced anywhere in the European provinces of Russia.

---

[9]Lantzeff, pp. 80–84.
[10]Ibid., p. 84; Arkheograficheskaia komissiia, *Dopolneniia k aktam istoricheskim* (Saint Petersburg, 1846–72), 3: 312.
[11]Lantzeff, p. 85.
[12]Ibid., p. 40. See Ogloblin, 3: 36 for other examples.

Such was the influence of the new frontier upon those who were assigned to tame and exploit this wilderness. Among more common folk the frontier conditions of Siberia produced unusual prospects for social mobility, unusual opportunities for personal achievement, and great rewards for strong and capable individuals. Sources for the study of the Siberian economy and Siberian society, though understandably sparse, confirm that Siberia, like frontiers everywhere, acknowledged and rewarded able individuals who could promote economic interests, provide effective leadership, and organize communities in the domination of their environment. Circumstances of everyday life in Siberia made this necessary. Like Kievan Rus, Siberia was exposed to dangers so constant that often the total resources of communities had to be pooled for survival. When Kalmyk forces threatened the Tobolsk region in 1647, all classes and ranks of the local populace were pressed into service for the defense of their homes. To resist the siege that was expected, cossacks and other professional military servitors were reinforced by townspeople, peasants, artisans, and other menial laborers. All these were given assignments for the defense of the town. Even certain ecclesiastics were summoned to military service.[13] This common crisis and its democratic response undoubtedly fostered a spirit of equality among the inhabitants of Tobolsk and engendered feelings of camaraderie among all classes of people.

Class structure in Siberia was not so rigid and inflexible as it was west of the Urals. Although the highest levels of society (the *voevoda,* chief officials of government, and other important nobles) formed a privileged group because of their appointments by Moscow, these comprised the only stratum of Siberian life into which access could not be had by commoners. Throughout the rest of society, mobility and advancement based upon personal accomplishment were much in evidence. Individuals having needed skills were often appointed to the ranks of the military or given official positions (such as in the postal service). Those who distinguished themselves in military engagements or who demonstrated bravery or fine military manner were raised to the service class of garrisons, whereupon they acquired privileged status and the grants of lands that accompanied this distinction. Similar opportunities were available to the "wandering people" who migrated to Siberia illegally and who derived from diverse segments of Muscovite society.[14] As had been true of Kievan Rus, individuals from the lowest ranks of society found it possible to rise from the

[13]Slovtsov, 1: 65–66.
[14]Lantzeff, p. 203.

humblest antecedents to prominent position in their communities through ability and determination alone.

Labor of high quality and unusual industry was also rewarded with privileges that had been unknown in European Russia for centuries. Even as late as the eighteenth century workingmen in Siberia who possessed valuable skills were treated with greater deference by their political superiors and were accorded unusual preferment. Some highly skilled and badly needed workers were exempted from military recruitment. Often employers of such key laborers were obliged by the state to pay their poll tax, discharge their other financial dues, and make their economic position attractive.[15] Inasmuch as competition for such workers among towns and individual employers was keen, such craftsmen enjoyed great bargaining power. Like the foreign specialists who had been so indispensable to Muscovite society, they were above considerations that limited the opportunities of men of less ability.

Outside of the main garrison towns of Siberia, it was not uncommon for peasants, simple merchants, and others of low birth and humble occupation to reach positions of civic power and social prominence. Self-made men were found in positions of responsibility in many villages. In places where agricultural production was a severe problem, government officials often relied upon new "wandering people" to populate their farming tracts. These peasants were settled upon extensive parcels of land, were forgiven taxes, and were declared exempt from all service obligations for a certain period. Thereafter they were expected to share their harvests with the servitors of nearby garrisons or to plow land for the sole use of local authorities. Once financed and launched in these occupations by the state, many of these farmers were able to acquire additional land and considerable capital. Some developed into the sort of wealthy middle-class farmer the Russians later termed *kulak*. As their business prospered, some branched out into moneylending and other financial activities.

As early as the sixteenth century prosperous farmers of this variety had come to rule isolated villages in Siberia as quasi satraps of the Muscovite government. As their wealth and experience increased, some founded new villages and farming communities, where they functioned as mayors and representatives of the state. Some scholars have speculated that such enterprising individuals founded as many villages in Siberia as did the Muscovite government. One privately founded village in the district of Mangazeia comprised sixteen peasant households and was suffi-

[15] Mavor, 1: 499.

ciently wealthy to raise R1,500 for the construction of a village church.[16] Such were the prospects that Siberia offered those enterprising enough to dare the initial challenge of entering a new land devoid of means and patrons.

How those of extreme ability could rise to historical fame and fortune is perhaps best illustrated by the career of Erofei P. Khabarov, the Russian conqueror of the Amur Region. Khabarov migrated to Siberia in 1636, where he became an indepent farmer of the *kulak* variety described above. His sound business sense (he previously had owned and operated a saltworks in the Urals region before his departure for Siberia) suggested to him a number of private enterprises that proved to be quite lucrative. He discovered new arable lands, petitioned Moscow for peasants to work these lands, and created a number of productive farming communities. He then began to function as a true capitalist, renting farm equipment to those who lacked their own. Khabarov then turned to the fur trade, working as a *promyshlennik* himself, then hiring his own trappers and hunters. When Russian settlers entered the Lena River basin, Khabarov moved to the upper Lena and founded there new farming settlements. But he had his hand in many other rewarding businesses as well, renting horses and boats to local colonists, opening systems of transportation, and selling goods imported from Russia. He also founded a saltworks, which the government later confiscated for its own use.[17]

The Amur region attracted Khabarov's attention for its farming land, which was rich enough to provide a strong agricultural base for all Russian operations throughout eastern Siberia. Securing permission from the *voevoda* of Yakutsk, Khabarov mounted a private expedition into the Amur area with 150 *promyshlenniki* and military servitors in 1649. After he convinced Russian authorities of the riches and strategic value of the Amur, Khabarov was given 3,000 military men and the command to gather *yasak* along the Amur. His struggles with the Manchu rulers of China, his intrepid exploration of the Amur, and his reports on the importance of the Amur basin cause him to be remembered as one of the great explorers in Russian history. Following his expedition he was elevated to the middle service class and was appointed administrator of the fortress of Ilimsk.[18] His humble origins had not hindered him in his quest for riches and glory. Khabarov's great aptitude would have availed him

[16]P. N. Butsinsky, *Mangazeia i mangazeiskii uezd, 1601–1645 gg.* (Kharkov, 1893), pp. 32–35; Lantzeff, pp. 172–73.

[17]Lantzeff and Pierce, pp. 159–60.

[18]Ibid., pp. 160–67.

little in other parts of the Russian Empire. On the Siberian frontier these traits ensured his greatness.

The frontier influences of Siberia can also be seen upon the Siberian *Prikaz,* which developed many characteristics at variance with staid Muscovite administrative procedure. After the *promyshlenniki* and the cossacks had secured their hold upon Siberia and the financial benefits of the *yasak* had become known in Moscow, the Russian government created a separate Siberian *Prikaz* (or Siberian Office) to administer Siberian affairs and to deal with all problems of its settlement and exploitation. Usually the various *prikazy* of the Muscovite state system concerned themselves merely with implementing state policy within their jurisdictions and enforcing centralization and standardization throughout the empire. The Siberian *Prikaz,* because of its unique situation and the government's total lack of knowledge of conditions in the east, allowed local officials in Siberia to display a great deal of personal initiative in discharging their duties. Moscow's administration of Siberia became unique and contrasted sharply with normal practices.[19]

Because the Siberian *Prikaz* had among its duties the regulation of the rich traffic in furs from Siberia, its staff included many specialists in business affairs who were different in their attitudes and values from the bureaucratic functionaries who controlled the other *prikazy.* These men understood the potential riches to be reaped from the east and were quick to subordinate centralization, conformity, and other bureaucratic concerns to the realization of profit. For this reason the Siberian *Prikaz* solicited and received thousands of petitions from Siberian natives, servitors, settlers, and *promyshlenniki,* in order to obtain local points of view and to receive suggestions on how things could be better managed. Among these petitions were many letters complaining of abuses in local administration and pleas for assistance of every kind. The *prikaz* sent its own special investigators to Siberia to recommend changes in policy and to investigate reported abuses of authority.[20] At one point the archives of the *prikaz* contained more than twenty thousand individual reports from officials in Siberia concerning local needs, problems, and prospects.[21]

The Muscovite government seemed well aware that the unique conditions of the Siberian frontier might make their mark upon Russian institutions and loosen the hold of the state over its subjects. To avoid such influence, Moscow decreed in 1695 and again in 1696 that other *prikazy*

[19]S. Prutchenko, *Sibirskiia okrainy* (Saint Petersburg, 1899), 1: 11.
[20]Lantzeff, p. 18; Ogloblin, 3: 87.
[21]Ogloblin, 3: 2.

and individuals were not to circumvent the Siberian *Prikaz* and deal directly with Siberian settlements and their administrators. Severe punishments were promised violators of this command.[22] Thus, the Siberian *Prikaz,* while encouraging initiative and self-sufficiency in Siberia, acted as a filter in which the potentially disruptive elements of Siberian life and service were removed before their entry into Great Russia. The frontier spirit of Siberia affected the Siberian *Prikaz* itself but remained localized within its offices.

Barred from access to Russia proper, the restless energy of the Siberian frontiersman worked its way progressively eastward toward the Pacific. With the passage of time, however, only the far eastern regions of the Siberian expanses remained free of Russian control. By the mid-seventeenth century, service men in Siberia had begun to view the Amur basin as their last haven from the disciplined life in their garrisons. During the 1650s hundreds of military servitors and cossacks deserted their posts and made their way to the Amur. Their ranks were swelled by exiles, runaway peasants, and the ubiquitous *promyshlenniki.* In 1655 the *voevoda* of the town of Ilimsk calculated that about fifteen hundred deserters from lands under his authority had relocated to the banks of the Amur.[23]

Some cossacks, wishing to recreate the life they had known or had heard of on the steppe, tried to create their own settlements in the Amur region patterned on earlier cossack models. In 1665 an exiled Pole, Nikifor Chernigovsky, led a group of disgruntled cossacks to the Amur, where he erected a series of forts and blockhouses along tributaries of the river. For seven years thereafter Chernigovsky and his men enjoyed new autonomy in a sovereign republic, known as Albazin, that recognized no overlordship. This attempt to return to the traditional habits of the independent cossack community was doomed by the onward march of Muscovite hegemony. In 1672 government detachments reached Chernigovsky's stronghold and subordinated his small republic to Moscow.[24] But even under Muscovite sovereignty Chernigovsky's cossacks continued a lawless life that gravely complicated the delicate relations between Russia and China in the Amur district. Chernigovsky's followers were so vicious in extorting tribute from local tribes subject to the Manchu emperor that these tribesmen appealed to China for assistance. After numerous complaints to Chernigovsky, all of which remained

[22]*Polnoe sobranie zakonov rossiiskoi imperii s 1649 goda.* 1st ser. (Saint Petersburg, 1830), 3: 206, 266–68; Lantzeff, pp. 14–15.

[23]N. N. Ogloblin, "Bunt i pobeg na Amur vorovskogo polka M. Sorokina," *Russkaia starina* 85 (1896): 206–12.

[24]S. V. Bakhrushin, *Kazaki na Amure,* p. 167.

unanswered, Chinese forces surrounded Albazin in 1685, killed many of its cossacks, and forced the settlement to surrender. The Chinese allowed the Russian survivors to retreat to Nerchinsk, then razed this nest of cossackdom on the Amur.[25]

Chernigovsky's cossacks were emulated by many of the native inhabitants of Siberia. As Russian administrators and servitors increased their efforts to wring from the natives tribute in fur, the native populace imitated Russian malcontents by fleeing en masse to far eastern territories. The Amur became the last frontier for these refugees.[26] But the signing of the Treaty of Nerchinsk between Russia and China on August 21, 1689, barred Russian settlers from the entire Amur valley. The loss of the Amur region, where agricultural yield had promised to be very high, dealt a serious blow to Russian operations east of Lake Baikal. Because the area between Baikal and the Amur was very poor for farming, Russian enterprisers in that region had to rely upon hunting and trapping for their livelihood. The population of these parts remained much smaller than would have been the case had the agricultural base of the Amur been placed at their disposal. Until modern times, therefore, Russian settlements east of Lake Baikal have retained their frontier character, because of the nomadic occupations forced upon their inhabitants by lack of arable land.[27] But the loss of the Amur closed Russia's last safety valve. Thereafter prospects for flight from the encroaching institutionalization of life became considerably dimmer.

The Russian government was never able to destroy fully the taste for freedom and self-reliance of its frontier subjects in Siberia. Indeed, attempts to do so were halfhearted at best. But Moscow did realize another important objective. A vast new colony was appended to the Russian Empire, while the frontier spirit of that colony was prevented from influencing the development of national institutions in the Russian heartland. The center of the Russian state continued beneath the governance of the principles of autocracy, serfdom, and service first enunciated by the grand princes of Moscow. Only in more remote places did memories of personal liberty and dreams of individualism survive. Distance has always been the great protector of the Russian state system. In later years the frontier made its mark upon Russian history only in a violent and self-destructive manner. The peasant upheavals of Bulavin and Pugachev challenged the Russian establishment only for a brief time. In the end they were defeated by the advanced technology and discipline that

[25]Golder, pp. 55–60.
[26]Lantzeff, pp. 109–10.
[27]Lantzeff and Pierce, pp. 181–82.

centrally administered societies claim as their raison d'etre. Eastern Siberia has continued to experience a greater degree of personal freedom
and opportunity that has survived even Stalin. But between these
frontiersmen and the Russian center lay an artificially created buffer
zone: the regulated, institutionalized tracts of western Siberia, which
absorbed and assimilated all manifestations of the frontier spirit before
they could cross the Urals and unsettle Russian national life.

IX. The Legacy of the Frontier in Russian History

DEFENDERS of the Muscovite state system have often argued that the inhabitants of Russian borderlands, such as the cossacks, have traditionally stood for license, unbridled passion, violence, and barbarism. The Russian political and social system, on the other hand, with all its repression and restraint, has represented law and order, peace and security, and the gradual attainment, at least by a select elite, of the benefits of enlightenment and civilization. Others have affirmed that, given the imperfect nature of any social order, discrimination against, and oppression of, minorities are inevitable. This group finds it far more just to all segments of society to base political and social principles upon the tenets of the service state, a comprehensive and stern political organism that compels all ranks and all classes of the citizenry, even the tsar himself, to serve the common good. Writing of the retrenchment of serfdom that followed the Time of Troubles, William McNeill described this attitude with clarity: "If government were inescapable and an evil—as Russian along with all other peasants no doubt felt—at least the autocratic, Orthodox tsar, as mirrored forth once more by Michael Romanov, was an intelligible power-wielder. His oppressions were the more tolerable because he oppressed everyone, rich and poor, landholder and cultivator, merchant and soldier." [1]

Russian nationalists of the nineteenth century, and particularly the Slavophiles, saw in the notion of strong autocratic power not only a preferable system of rule but one of the fundamental national virtues that distinguished Russian political life from that of all other peoples. Monarchists everywhere have raised similar justifications for austere centralized government, citing man's debased and fallen nature as the reason for the necessity of absolute rule. Left to his own devices, conservatives have always maintained, man can only debase all values that he encounters and work his ruin and that of all he encounters.

This study makes no pretensions of casting moral judgments upon the

---

[1] William H. McNeill, *Europe's Steppe Frontier, 1500–1800* (Chicago: University of Chicago Press, 1964), p. 84.

particular course of history that has been surveyed within these pages. Each reader will answer the moral questions that history raises in his own way. It is true, however, that the history of the Russian frontier lands, from the far north to the southern steppe to the far reaches of Siberia and the Russian far east, are filled with enough violence, rapacity, and depravity to support the contention that these were lands where uncivilized segments of society congregated to escape the principles of law and the basic dictates of the norms of morality. What we see in Russian history, however, is not the contest between moral and immoral, or humane and barbaric, forces, but a protracted struggle between two principles: the orderly but repressive state mechanism against the free but unlicensed frontiersman. Both principles were given extreme expression in Russia. The Russian state was as immoderate in its oppressions as the cossacks, the *ushkuiniki* and the *promyshlenniki* were unbridled in their activities. The tragedy of Russian history is that never did Moscow devise a means of moderating national abuses and mediating national extremes. Inflexible in its own self-righteousness, the Russian government continued to propagate its own abuses while lamenting and opposing contrary abuses in its opponents. The synthesis between the law and order of the state and the freedom and enterprise of the frontier was never achieved. Instead, the two antagonists continued to oppose each other and struggled to prevent a defeat that would destroy the extremes each one favored. Whether one applauds or condemns the final outcome of this struggle will depend upon one's conception of the philosophy of history and one's view of human nature.

With Peter the Great's implementation of the full ideals of the service state and Catherine the Great's annexation of the Crimea and absorption of the southern cossack communities, the open conflict between the Russian state and the lands of the frontier came to an end. Siberia still offered promise of an escape from the stringencies of Russian national life. But by Catherine's day the Siberian lands had been tamed of much of their primitive violence and, because of the iron curtain that western Siberia provided, no longer posed a threat to the Muscovite system. Yet it would be erroneous to believe that the influence of the Russian frontier had reached its end. By the end of the eighteenth century the Russian government had conquered the sort of frontier that Turner had seen in the American West, a positive force that could militate against the established values of the capital and transform its way of life. That sort of frontier Russia would not see again. But there were more subtle, though no less important, ways in which the Russian borderlands influenced the course of Russian history. And we should be rash to suppose that these influences will not be felt again in our own day.

Throughout the nineteenth century Moscow continued to use Siberia as a safety valve for its own purposes. The Decembrists were the first of a number of political enemies whose resettlement to wastelands was undertaken as a means of removing dangerous elements from the centers of state power. Toward the end of the century it became customary for foreigners and enemies of the regime to depict the Siberian exile system as unenlightened and brutal. Yet some communities of exiles were actually accorded a high degree of personal freedom that gave them exposure to their fellow residents in Siberia and frequent opportunity to exert significant influence upon the development of local Siberian life.[2] It was not uncommon for exiles to Siberia to acquire high status and personal enrichment despite their supposed imprisonment. Some became owners of mines, practiced the higher professions, and conducted business of many sorts. Because most exiles knew little of agriculture, they remained a volatile and diverse element that added a strong discordant note to the populace. After the suppression of the Polish revolution of 1863, many exiled Poles with broad education and important skills also joined their ranks. The intelligentsia of many a Siberian town was composed of such political dissidents and social revolutionaries.[3]

When overpopulation and socialist agitation later threatened to upset the countryside of European Russia, these intellectuals were joined in Siberia by simpler folk who, like the "wandering people" of earlier times, traded unsatisfactory homesites west of the Urals for new surroundings. The two million peasants who followed Stolypin's advice and migrated to Siberia were another example of the conscious determination of the Russian government to relegate potentially troublesome groups to the frontier. Here their energy could be devoted to struggles with nature, and their desire for personal betterment could reap important new harvests for the good of the state.

Throughout the second half of the nineteenth century and the first years of the twentieth, the settlers of Siberia, whatever their origins, exhibited not only a greater disposition toward full democracy in their native village assemblies but greater self-reliance, initiative, and willingness to experiment with new methods and aids to agriculture. Cooperatives,

   [2]V. M. Zenzinov and I. D. Levine, *The Road to Oblivion* (London: R. M. McBride and Co., 1932).
   [3]Terence E. Armstrong, *Russian Settlement in the North* (Cambridge: Cambridge University Press, 1965), p. 84.

credit unions, and similar agencies of self-help were prevalent, in tes-
timony to the desire of the populace to better itself through joint efforts
and common endeavor. Individualism was everywhere noticeable in Siberia. Although democracy was precluded by the autocratic regime that
maintained the pan-national institutions of the Russian Empire, the
people of Siberia developed many traits that have prepared the land much
better for democracy than have any measures adopted by the Soviet
regime.[4] This circumstance may yet prove important in Russian political
life of the future.

Siberian life was also given greater diversity by the continuous influx of
religious dissidents that continued throughout the nineteenth century.
The *skoptsy* (castrates) appeared in Siberia first during the reign of
Catherine the Great and by 1860 had formed a large and highly efficient
agricultural community in the Yakutsk area. The Yakutsk region, like
certain other sections of Siberia, became a haven for schismatics and har-
bored significant communities of Old Believers until late in the nineteenth
century. Near the end of the century the Christian anarchists known as
the Doukhobors also settled near Yakutsk. Fewer in numbers and less
influential than other schismatics, they nevertheless added their own
leaven of diversity and nonconformity to Siberian life until the 1890s,
when they departed for a new frontier in Canada.[5] All these religious
rebels lived their lives outside the bounds of the Russian state system and
refused adherence to its principles or service to its institutions.

It would perhaps be rewarding to enumerate the important social
rebels against the tsarist system who were born and reared in the Russian
borderlands. Chernyshevsky, Plekhanov, Trotsky, Lenin, and a host of
lesser-known members of the Russian revolutionary movement derived
from regions that had formed the Russian frontier at a comparatively late
point in history and where dreams of freedom and spontaneity of life were
far from forgotten.[6] Although Moscow triumphed in its efforts to achieve
political control of its outlying provinces, the Russian dream of total
Russification of the empire was never realized to any appreciable degree
in outlying areas. Despite all the attention given projects of assimilation
and cultural leveling by Alexander III, Pobedonostsev, and Nicholas II,

[4]Donald W. Treadgold, *The Great Siberian Migration: Government and Peasant in Resettlement from Emancipation to the First World War* (Princeton: Princeton University Press, 1957), p. 244–45.

[5]Armstrong, pp. 91–93.

[6]For this suggestion I am indebted to Professor Serge Zenkovsky of Vanderbilt University.

much of the Russian Empire, and especially Siberia, remained a vast melting pot of nationalities, religious beliefs, and ethnic customs. On the eve of the revolutions of 1917 the population of Siberia was less than ten million people, of which about one hundred thousand were non-Russian. These native nationalities, the descendants of those who had paid the *yasak* to the *promyshlenniki* and the cossacks, spurned modernization and industrialization and continued a nomadic life based upon fishing, hunting, and the raising of animals. Less than 10 percent of these indigenous folk could speak Russian but relied upon clan elders and other intermediaries to conduct their business with representatives of the commercial and political interests of the Russian government. Many of these people even continued to practice forms of paganism and shamanism, much to the dismay of the Russian church.[7] We need not wonder why so many of the prominent revolutionaries banished to Siberia by the tsarist government managed to escape their exile so easily. In such surroundings the power of Moscow, which was so heavyhanded elsewhere, must have been tenuous indeed.

During the first revolution of 1917, the provisional government that replaced tsar Nicholas II was right in saying that its coup was one that had been "made by telegraph." One provincial town after another had relayed its approval of Nicholas's removal and the transition to professedly more democratic forms of government. Dissatisfaction with the Romanov dynasty was strong throughout Russia; even stronger in outlying areas was the endemic and spontaneous hostility to all the power concentrated in Petrograd and Moscow, a hostility that was founded upon long memories of Muscovite efforts toward centralization, Russification, and assimilation. For similar reasons the Bolshevik revolutions met only isolated and sporadic opposition in the frontier sectors of Russia. Lenin's promises that the state would wither away, that peasants and workers would receive new autonomy, and that non-Russian nationalities would achieve self-determination corresponded with many of the fondest wishes of the people of the borderlands. When Lenin's early months in power demonstrated his unwillingness to create freer forms of government and society in Russia, those who lived beyond the reach of his police and party functionaries were not slow to reject his authority and to ally with more democratic opponents of the Soviet regime.

The Russian civil war that followed was a classic confrontation between the traditional forces of Muscovy and the rebelliousness of the frontier

[7]Liashchenko, pp. 598–99.

lands. When one examines a map of Bolshevik and anti-Bolshevik territorial holdings at the start of the war, one is immediately struck by the realization that the area that remained under firm Bolshevik control corresponded almost exactly to the original heartland of the old Muscovite state, the ancient forest zone in which the temporary loss of frontiers occasioned by the Mongol yoke deprived Russia of broad horizons and facilitated the spread of serfdom and autocracy. The frontier territories and borderlands of the Russian Empire, including the vast expanses of Siberia, fell with relative ease beneath the sway of the Social Revolutionaries and other enemies of the Bolsheviks.[8] The reasons for the Red victory in this confrontation were identical to the reasons for the original triumph of the principality of Moscow over its rivals and neighbors. Hunger for freedom and independence was not enough in itself to ensure the triumph of the White armies. In the end the centralized, tightly organized, and rigidly disciplined Bolsheviks, using all the resources and institutions of the ancient center of the Russian state, crushed their opponents, just as Vasily Shuisky, tsar Alexis, and Catherine II had crushed Bolotnikov, Razin, and Pugachev.

But the Bolsheviks could not accomplish what had always eluded the tsars. Red forces were unable to win a military victory over the Russian far east, the last of the safety valves and the final refuge of the most discontented and adventurous members of Russian society. The bandit Seménov, a modern counterpart of Chernigovsky, created in the far east a sanctuary of autonomy from state control that proved so persistent in its opposition to rule from Moscow that the Bolsheviks had to agree to the formation of the Far Eastern Republic. As Lenin's hold on Russia became unbreakable, those who steadfastly refused him recognition fled eastward to the Republic, where, like Chernigovsky's garrison at Albazin, a few years of additional hope were allowed them. As Komarovsky says in *Doctor Zhivago,* before himself fleeing to the Republic: "Siberia—truly a new America, as it is often called—has immense possibilities. It is the cradle of Russia's future greatness, the gauge of our progress toward democracy and political and economic health."[9] But with the withdrawal of Japanese interventionists from Vladivostok and the consolidation of Bolshevik power throughout western Siberia, the Republic found no champion to pit against Muscovite strength. With the field to himself, Lenin was able to secure the political subordination of this last frontier in late 1922.

[8] Treadgold, "Russian Expansion," pp. 150–52.
[9] Boris Pasternak, *Doctor Zhivago* (New York: Pantheon, 1958), p. 424.

Throughout the years of Soviet rule the Siberian frontier has been a challenge and something of a mysterious force to Soviet leaders. The seemingly unlimited opportunities for private enterprise beyond the Urals and the relatively free atmosphere of Siberia have often attracted Soviet youth to exchange careers in European Russia for less constrained modes of life in the east. The call of Siberia has recently been heard again in the writings of Alexander Solzhenitsyn, who has suggested a return to the spirit of the Russian northeast through a new program of colonization and exploitation that will increase Russia's natural wealth and rekindle the spirit and enthusiasm of its people.[10] The vastness of the Siberian frontier and its underdevelopment are important factors in Russia's future. Whether this future will be marred by new frontier violence or enriched by some of the benefits provided America by its western frontier remains to be seen.

[10]See the *New York Times,* Mar. 3, 1974, pp. 1, 26.

Index

Index